A Story of Love

by Courtney G.

A Story of Love

Trilogy Christian Publishers A Wholly Owned Subsidiary of Trinity Broadcasting Network

2442 Michelle Drive Tustin, CA 92780

Rights Department, 2442 Michelle Drive, Tustin, CA 92780.

Trilogy Christian Publishing/TBN and colophon are trademarks of Trinity Broadcasting Network.

Cover design by: Kristy Swank

For information about special discounts for bulk purchases, please contact Trilogy Christian Publishing.

Trilogy Disclaimer: The views and content expressed in this book are those of the author and may not necessarily reflect the views and doctrine of Trilogy Christian Publishing or the Trinity Broadcasting Network.

Manufactured in the United States of America

10 9 8 7 6 5 4 3 2 1

Library of Congress Cataloging-in-Publication Data is available.

ISBN: 978-1-68556-865-8

E-ISBN: 978-1-68556-866-5

ACKNOWLEDGMENTS

When I first began my journey with Jesus, I had no idea what I was getting into. However, after many months of studying and researching, I finally understood how the most joyful people remain joyful throughout their journey. When I first wrote *A Story of Love*, my heart, hands, and head were all in the right place. I was focused on spreading the good news like a shepherd to the small groups I was leading at the time. However, a few short months later, my life looked drastically different. I wanted to continue sharing the good events that were happening in my life, but I was faced with heartache, betrayal, and loss. Not only did I feel alone along my journey, the enemy was taking that feeling and feeding me lies about my Father on the journey. So, I did what any woman does: filled with passion and emotion, I cried. Night after night, day after day, I sought Him and His presence, then I started reaching out to my sisters and brothers in Christ for help, and each person began to help me through prayer and listening.

These friends have kept me focused and encouraged throughout this new journey when I have felt overwhelmed and distracted, but each of them, through their own trials and triumphs, have contributed not only to me telling the story of Jesus but also contributing to my story with Jesus!

Mom and Dad: thank you for placing the Word of God in front of me each day and praying over me from before I was born.

Aunt Kathy: thank you for being just as excited as me on this journey! As well as helping, guiding, and encouraging me along the way. You have given me hugs

ACKNOWLEDGEMENTS

and held my hand more times than I can count, ensuring me I am doing what God has called me to do. (I also dedicate Day 17 in this book to you!)

Mallory, Kayla, Logan, Rachel, Kelly, Alexa, Rachel, Payton, Mary Kathryn, Rachel, Cara, Avery: thank you for encouraging me and being supportive through the late nights and early mornings, lack of energy, and constant pull back into the fold of friendship. I am blessed to have friends who push me toward the finish line.

Ashley, Jennifer, and Kathryn: thank you for helping me write this book. It was good knowing I had two faithful women of God teaching and correcting me through this new adventure.

Glenda and Grant, LaLania and Cary, Lisa and Tony, Elizabeth and David, Melissa and Jay, Vickie and Bobbie, Heather and Sean, Mellody and Scott, Diana and Dan, Aunt Nancy and Uncle Bill: I am truly blessed beyond measure to follow in the footsteps each of you have taken on your own journeys. Each of you has listened to me as I have poured out my heart and its desires, questions, and struggles. Thank you for helping me walk the righteous path and stay the course!

TABLE OF CONTENT

Preface	8
Introduction	9
Day 1: Joy with Us	11
Day 2: Plug In and Light Up!	17
Day 3: Joyfully Chop Away	23
Day 4: Branch Out	31
Day 5: Praying for a Gift	37
Day 6: Cherish Your Precious Gift	45
Day 7: Be Silent When God Speaks	53
Day 8: Highly Favored	61
Day 9: Decisions, Decisions	71
Day 10: Desires Demand Daily Devotions	77
Day 11: Joy-Filled Visitation	85
Day 12: Prayers: Praising and Proclaiming	91
Day 13: He Is with You on Your Journey	99
Day 14: Happy Birthday Jesus!	107
Day 15: Good News of Great Joy	113
Day 16: Peace Is on the Earth 65	117
Day 17: Be Where God Has Called You to Be	121

Day 18: The First Mission Trip   127

Day 19: Patience and Prayer   133

Day 20: Come and Worship Him   141

Day 21: Be Delighted, Not Disturbed   147

Day 22: Manipulation Is Not a Wise Move   153

Day 23: Drop It and Leave It   159

Day 24: Follow in Obedience   165

Day 25: It's Not Just Any Story; It's His Story   169

Day 26: Peace   173

About the Author   175

PREFACE

In the spirit of all things Christmas, it has been laid upon my heart to lead the generations through a journey of following love as Christ loved.

Listen to these words spoken by John over 2,000 years ago that we might cling to love, "For God so loved the world that he gave his one and only Son, that whoever believes in Him shall not perish but have eternal life" (John 3:16). Because our Heavenly Father is love, He sent His Son Jesus to come to our rescue. This was the ultimate act of love.

It is a comfort to cling to Truth through our days as we follow our lovely leader, Jesus. I pray that each day you will cling to this lovely story of a babe filled with so much love that He left a perfect place to come to a place of imperfections so that we would have an opportunity to follow love through our days.

We all desire to be loved. But have we slowed down enough to even begin to comprehend the true love that entered the world in the form of a baby wrapped in swaddling cloths? Have we considered the conflict and conversations, emotions, and thoughts of those who either helped or tried to hinder the coming of love (Jesus) into this world?

Come along with me as we venture through the Scriptures with the Holy Spirit and bring to light the most amazing account of love that ever was or ever will be again—when Love moved first.

INTRODUCTION

Have you ever been discouraged along your journey? I know the feeling too, friend. And truthfully, the journey gets long, exhausting, and overwhelming. Am I right? But due to our faith in the promises the Lord graciously gives, you and I can take the journey ahead and have that special time with the Lord this holiday season.

Day 1

Joy with Us

In the beginning was the Word, and the Word was with God, and the Word was God. He was with God in the beginning. Through Him all things were made; without Him nothing was made that has been made. In Him was life, and that life was the light of all mankind. The light shines in the darkness, and the darkness has not overcome it.

John 1:1–5

In the beginning…

It all begins where God started. Now, that may sound obvious to you, but this verse alongside Genesis 1:1, which states, "In the beginning God created the heavens and the earth" is profound in many more ways than one can ever comprehend. We see here, as we begin the journey of the birth of Jesus, John starts at the beginning. I am sure as he was writing, he could not decide where to begin. Much like myself, I wanted to start with the birth of Jesus, but I was quickly reminded that like any story, there are many moments that lead to where the climax of the story is.

My story does not start where you turned the page to today; joyfully and faithfully leading. In fact, it starts way before the pages of my life began. Like anyone before they enter into the world, each person is led in by family and family friends who will help lead, guide, and teach them through their own journey. I would not be who I am today had it not been for those who came before me to pave the way to teach me how to be a leader in life, joyful in the midst of trials and faithful in the times of weariness. And it does not surprise me that our merciful Heavenly Father did the same with His Son when He ushered grace into this world filled with darkness and depression. Yes, the miracle of Jesus entering through the birth of a virgin was a miracle, but the subtle conversations, prayers, and interactions that led to one of the greatest moments in history shouldn't be overlooked as miracles either. As we begin walking the journey of the birth of Jesus this holiday season, we are going to see how intimate God can be with those that He loves. After all, He did send His only Son into the world because He loved not only the world but also those that live in it. So, snuggle up, friend, grab that cozy blanket, a pen, and a notepad because you and I are about to learn more about God, man, and sin, as well as the love in Christ Jesus this holiday season. Trust me when I say we have quite a bit to cover. So just like John started at the beginning, I will do the same.

God knew there was no other way for His people to understand how to live in the world and not be of it. So, He not only created and acted upon the most brilliant plan that no man could ever think of doing (and certainly could never pull off) by making life out of Himself in the form of a human but, at the same time, He fulfilled His promise:

"Therefore, the Lord Himself will give you a sign: The virgin will conceive and give birth to a son, and will call Him Immanuel" (Isaiah 7:14).

Think about it like this for a moment: before Jesus entered the world and belted out His very first cry, God's people had not heard from Him in over 400 years! Can you imagine living during that time? Hearing people say over and over that the Lord is coming to save the people but not seeing any action taking place. I am not sure about you, but if I don't hear from God my Father for more than 400 minutes, my flesh starts to take over, and my Spirit is quenched. Can you imagine how the people must have felt and what they must have been thinking during this time? They were under the unjust rule of Rome and had already escaped from a life of captivity. In their misery and slavery, they must have questioned whether God was listening to their cries or concerns.

> *Lovely Encouragement:*
>
> God had a plan for His creation long before He created it. And since He had not communicated to them the timing of His plan, He fulfilled His promise with one word, Jesus.

There was no big moment that led to God being silent. Yet, in the time of God's silence, not only was He moving, but the enemy was on the move as well. Revelation 12:12 speaks about the enemy being filled with fury because he knows his time is short. However, 400 years is a long period of time, especially for the enemy to be moving and meddling. But little did the world know that while he was moving, tucked away in a trough lay the Word of God, already in motion.

God laid the biggest layup, threw the fastest pitch right down the center of the plate, and said "checkmate" to the father of lies!

But how did God do it? Instead of God sending His Son on a white horse, through the clouds and a trumpet sounding as His way to come save the world from deep darkness and despair, He sent Him to a quiet, poor family. He did not plug in a spotlight and shine His glory down so the world could see what He had done. God Himself, through the conception of the Holy Spirit and a virgin woman, gave a way for His Son to enter into the darkness and one day overcome it.

The light which John speaks about is not one that can be turned on or off. In fact, it is one that has been on since God spoke it into existence. It had always been inside and of Him, but He desired to expose it so the darkness (spiritual forces) could know that the battle had already been won. Satan stops at nothing to attempt to win, but the truth that we can find comfort in is that before we were even created, our Father had already prepared a way for our victory.

Lovely Encouragement:

God is the Father of lights (James 1:17)! Satan is the father of lies (John 8:44).

Today was only Day 1, and we may not have covered too much, but I encourage you to stay plugged in, my friends, as we continue to follow Jesus through His story. We are going to discover more about ourselves through the people who paved the way for us. We will look at the decisions they made based on the desires of their heart and the devotion they have with their Father.

Prayer: Father God, Creator of all things good, I thank You for who You are. Thank You that no matter what is going on in this world, ultimately, Your plans will be accomplished. Help me as Your child to keep my ear turned toward You so that I will not find myself sifting through the chaos or confusion but rather look to You for clarity. Thank You that I can trust You with Your timing all the days of my life. Thank You for sending Your sweet, saving Son into the darkness to help us follow You. I pray this in Your Son's precious, perfect, and powerful name, Jesus, amen!

Questions

» Are you aware that with every journey, you will undoubtedly be faced with hills, valleys, and even treacherous trails? And are you willing to put in the work for your journey that is set ahead for you?

» What characters do you hope to learn more about on this journey?

» Without looking, who do you think you are most like in the story of Jesus' birth?

» Also, without looking, who do you think you are least like in this Christmas story?

» Last question, what areas in your life do you need the light to shine through so you can walk out of the darkness and into the light?

Day 2

Plug In and Light Up!

The people walking in darkness have seen a great light; on those living in the land of deep darkness a light has dawned. You have enlarged the nation and increased their joy; they rejoice before You as people rejoice at the harvest, as warriors rejoice when dividing the plunder. For as in the day of Midian's defeat, You have shattered the yoke that burdens them, the bar across their shoulders, the rod of their oppressor. Every warrior's boot used in battle and every garment rolled in blood will be destined for burning, will be fuel for the fire. For to us a child is born, to us a son is given, and the government will be on His shoulders. And He will be called Wonderful Counselor, Mighty God, Everlasting Father, Prince of Peace. Of the greatness of His government and peace there will be no end. He will reign on David's throne and over his kingdom, establishing and upholding it with justice and righteousness from that time on and forever. The zeal of the Lord Almighty will accomplish this.

Isaiah 9:2–7

As we read from John 1 on Day 1, we saw the Word of God, who was Jesus, become the light for all mankind (See Genesis 1:2). As we follow and learn to connect Christ through this Christmas season, there is one thing that I think we can relate to with this talk of light: Christmas lights! Those twinkling lights we see on rooftops, trees, windows. They are everywhere! Those lights are there to grab our attention and let you and I see their beauty in the darkness.

If you know anything about electricity, it is the flow of charge. Inside those Christmas lights are wires that send electrons in an orderly fashion that let you sense the excitement of the Christmas season. After you have dragged out that box of lights from the attic and untangled them for what seems like hours on end, you plug them in to begin the experience of the holiday season. However, what happens when you unplug those twinkling lights, not only do you not experience that warm and fuzzy feeling of Christmas anymore, but you are right back where you were, in the darkness without a beautiful light. When we step away or unplug ourselves from the Word, we become disconnected, leaving our lights turned off and dark.

Here is the beautiful part of the story: when you engage and plug yourself into Scripture, lessons, memorizing Scripture, and begin the conversations with God again, your light turns back on. It sounds so simple. And truthfully it is. Isaiah gave us the names of Jesus so we can plug ourselves into Him during those dark days or times. And we can have what we need to see through the darkness.

Lovely Encouragement:

Wonderful Counselor: Your Father wants you to talk to Him. He is your greatest Counselor and will give you wise advice no matter the circumstance.

Mighty God: He is stronger than your greatest weakness. And He is most definitely stronger than you. He desires for you to come to Him when you are weak so He can give you what you need for the situation(s) at hand.

Everlasting Father: He is your Father. He genuinely loves you for who you are because you are His. He created you and knit you together. No father's love on earth can compare to the love of the Father who is everlasting.

Prince of Peace: He desires peace in the world and in your relationship with Him.

There was a time in my life when I allowed my light to dim and then eventually disconnect. It didn't start off with an immediate unplugging, but over time I realized that darkness was all around me. You see, my dad left me and my sister's lives during my senior year of high school. My sister passed away a few years later, and my future was not going the way I had hoped, and I had just forfeited my future for my faith. These events did not happen overnight;

19

it was more like a span of ten years, but in those long and pressing years, the love I once knew was dimming. I wanted nothing more than to focus on myself and fix my own problems. That was until a woman of God walked into the salon I was working at and shined a light into my dark world.

After about a year, my light was turning back on. I began to have a family, but not the traditional kind you would think. This was a family of all ages, races, lifestyles. I began getting connected to people who were connected to the Word. All my life, I made it a responsibility to go to church every Sunday to remain a responsible daughter of God. But I was missing something. I did not have a relationship with Jesus. After years of watching women walk through life, I began to understand how to stay connected to Jesus even through the trials of abandonment, passing away of loved ones, and career changes. It made sense to me, but only because I stayed connected.

The truth is, Jesus is not a strand of lights. In fact, He calls Himself the Vine. Take a look with me here:

"Remain in Me, as I also remain in you. No branch can bear fruit by itself; it must remain in the vine. Neither can you bear fruit unless you remain in Me. I am the vine; you are the branches. If you remain in Me and I in you, you will bear much fruit; apart from Me you can do nothing"

John 15:4–5

> ## Lovely Encouragement:
>
> To me, a strand of lights resembles that of a vine. And when we remain (abide, stay connected), we too get the flow of charge we need to be able to shine bright, not only for ourselves to see but also for others.

The next time you drive by the home that is covered in lights or walk into your own home with lights around the Christmas tree and porch, remind yourself to remain in His Word so you can continue walking in the light.

Prayer: Gracious Heavenly Father, thank You for being the source of joy. I am truly grateful for who You are. I am blessed to be able to remain faithful in Your Word, which charges me and sends a constant flow of joy in the midst of every circumstance. Thank You for also sending Your Son, the Light, into this dark world to help us better see You. It is a comfort to know that You can never be unplugged, put in a box, or placed in the attic. You are not a seasonal God. You are a constant God. Thank You for being the source of the Wonderful Counselor, Mighty God, Everlasting Father, Prince of Peace. I pray this in the name of Jesus, amen.

Questions

» How many times a week are you plugged into the Word? (Circle one) 1 2 3 4 5 6 7

» Are you plugged into a community that believes the Bible and teaches it?

» Are you plugged into a small group that helps you stay accountable during this journey?

» If you do not have a church home or small group that you attend weekly, I would encourage you to begin praying that the church home and community you need to remain in would come available for you. It is good to read the Bible every day. However, you also need accountability from other believers to help you stay the course.

Day 3

Joyfully Chop Away

A shoot will come up from the stump of Jesse; from his roots a Branch will bear fruit. The Spirit of the Lord will rest on him—the Spirit of wisdom and of understanding, the Spirit of counsel and of might, the Spirit of the knowledge and fear of the Lord—and he will delight in the fear of the Lord. He will not judge by what he sees with his eyes or decide by what he hears with his ears; but with righteousness he will judge the needy, with justice he will give decisions for the poor of the earth. He will strike the earth with the rod of his mouth; with the breath of his lips he will slay the wicked. Righteousness will be his belt and faithfulness the sash around his waist. The wolf will live with the lamb, the leopard will lie down with the goat, the calf and the lion and the yearling together; and a little child will lead them. The cow will feed with the bear, their young will lie down together, and the lion will eat straw like the ox. The infant will play near the cobra's den, and the young child will put its hand into the viper's nest. They will neither harm nor destroy on all my holy mountain, for the earth will be filled with the knowledge of the Lord as the waters cover the sea. In that day the Root of Jesse will stand as a banner for the peoples; the nations will rally to him, and his resting place will be glorious.

Isaiah 11:1–10

The first person to have the idea to bring a Christmas tree into the house was a man named Martin Luther. In the sixteenth century, Martin Luther, who was a German preacher, took a stroll through the forest one evening. He took a gander at the sky and saw the stars shining through the silhouettes of the trees. He saw God's creation and desired to have that same feeling in his home, so he did something about it. He chopped a tree down and brought it home to his family. When Martin dragged the tree inside, his children were confused as to why their father would bring a tree into the home when a tree is meant to be outdoors. Martin took the opportunity at hand and told his family the beautiful story of Jesus. He expressed to his family that this tree was beautiful and it reminded him of Jesus. Therefore, just like Jesus, Martin wanted his family to gaze upon the beauty of the tree outside but also within the walls of his home. He explained the story of Christmas using God's creation and pointed out the love Jesus has for His people. Jesus did the same for you and me, He left a beautiful, perfect place to come and dwell within our home. (See 2 Corinthians 4:6–7.)

Christmas trees are a staple in homes around the holidays, if you think about it: every December (like Martin), we head to the forest, tree farm, or our local store to find the best tree that satisfies our eyes. Whether you go the traditional trail and have a real tree in your home or assemble the pieces to have the tree to your liking, we are all hoping for that same pleasant and peaceful look throughout our homes. For several decades, many of us have taken a liking to artificial trees. We have liked them for many reasons; they don't have to be maintained, they last for years, and we can manipulate the branches to our desire. Yet, on the flipside, many like the natural trees. The ones grown

24

in the soil are chopped in order to let them experience the joy in the Christmas season. Which tree do you sway toward? If you are anything like me, you have the artificial tree but truly desire the traditional Christmas tree. I'll let you in on a little secret on the reason: I am not a great gardener. Or I should say, I am not a great waterer. As a matter of fact, I once killed an aloe. However, that does not stop my heart from desiring a real plant or tree in my home around the holidays.

All this talk about trees; let's take a look at the one we read from today's scripture. (See Isaiah 11:1–10.) Isaiah speaks about how Assyria would be like a tree that would eventually be cut down at the height of its power and never rise again. The Lord gave them this promise not to worry them but to give them hope. His desire was for Judah to rest in Him through the trials of the Assyrians and their judgment. The Assyrians were cruel and ruthless men who were famous for being an intimidating army. Fighting was their way of life, and it was how they survived. God even spoke through Isaiah and called the Assyrians the rod of His anger (Isaiah 10:5). God did in fact say those words. Could you imagine God saying that about you and your family?

Yet, the Lord desired a real relationship with His people. And within that desire, He longs for us to live a holy and whole life with Him. That is why He spoke through Isaiah and said, "A shoot will come up from the stump." God said this to give comfort and hope to His people. This stump was not a stem or a dead log; it had roots, roots that ran deep. (See Matthew 1:1–17.) Jesse's roots could not be removed to start a new tree. That is why Jesus met His creations right where they were and became what they needed. And He does the same for us today.

The remnant left from this stump was an eye-opener to those living in Judah. You see, they knew they were going to be praised. (See Genesis 49:8–12.) This was a promise God made about Judah (the royal line of David). He wrote that this tree would be chopped down to a stump, which you see in verse 1, and then, the miraculous and most lovely shoot would grow from that foundation—the Messiah!

Now, let's take a travel into another woman's life, Ruth. You may know her by the book that is written about part of her life! Now, if you are a Bible lover like I am, you will notice the correlation between Ruth 4:18–22 and Matthew 1:1–16. Go check it out for yourself! What is something you noticed? Was it perhaps that David is in the line of the Messiah as well as Ruth? Therefore, we learn David is in the same family tree as Jesus the Messiah!

Lovely Encouragement:

Wild God Chase! 3-2-1! Genesis 49:8–12
Ruth 4:18–22 Matthew 1:1–16

Also did you catch that wording, "family tree?" There is no such thing as coincidences; God's words are so fascinating. Now, c'mon! We all deny things in life, but there is no denying God or His promises. We do not have to look too deep into this verse and see the backbone of God moving on behalf of His promises and people.

> *Lovely Encouragement:*
>
> God fulfilling this one promise should bring us pure joy!

Okay, so you are probably wondering how in the world these stories of our Messiah and Martin Luther connect. Well, I am glad you brought that up. As each of these trees was chopped down to their stumps, they bore beauty and boldness. God knew by allowing the people of Judah to be brought low, He Himself could lift them, grow them, and bless them beyond their wildest imagination. It may have taken judgment from others for them to root themselves into some truthful promises. And I am sure it was a long, hard, and challenging process. However, when they saw the fruit, from the shoot of the root, they praised God, and their brothers praised them, just as it was prophesied. (See Genesis 49:8.)

> *Lovely Encouragement:*
>
> You can't have fruit shoot if there is no root.

We have an opportunity to be a part of a growth process with Jesus. It takes courage to let God chop away what is harming us to see His beauty both within and around us. The desires and dreams or even the doubts are what hold us from growing with and in Jesus Christ. It could also be because we let our own dreams and desires take growth in our heart and what we end up with is something that needs to be chopped down and begin growing humbly, as Jesus did.

Since we are becoming friends, I will let you in on ways I have let my own desires take growth. I once dreamt I would be married, have a house full of children, teaching young minds and hearts knowledge of the world and the Word. And then, all of a sudden, I was chopped. I was brought low, as low as one can on a second-story apartment building. As I lay prostrate on the floor, tears flowing from my eyes, I released my desires and dreams into the hands of my Father. I remember feeling relief. In those excruciating and elongated moments of my release, I was emptied. I gave permission to God to remove what I had tried to grow on my own. Once I was "chopped," out of my stump grew a shoot, and from that shoot, I bore fruit. Well, how do we know if we have been chopped down and are growing fruit? When you grow with Christ, you begin showing Christ.

Lovely Encouragement:

Fruits that will shoot from you root—love, joy, peace, patience, kindness, goodness, faithfulness, gentleness, self-control, and more.

I urge you, dear sister, to allow the one who created you to chop what does not resemble Him so you can officially grow with and in Him. I would love to see your branches bearing sweet fruits that are stemmed from the same root as David!

Prayer: Abba Father, You are glorious. Your beauty can be seen in Your creation. I am thankful for what You desire of me. I give You permission to begin their pruning process. It is a privilege and honor to have You be my beautiful Gardener. Bless me with Your Presence, so I know I am not alone in this process, and You are doing this for me to look more like Your beautiful Branch, Jesus. I am weak, and I need help. I pray You grant me what I ask in the name of Jesus Christ, amen.

If you need help with where to start because you are afraid to let go of some branches or, better yet, being chopped down, please don't hesitate to reach out to someone you know is growing in the Lord to help you grow in Christ!

Day 4

Branch Out

"The days are coming," declares the Lord, "when I will fulfill the good promise I made to the people of Israel and Judah. In those days and at that time I will make a righteous Branch sprout from David's line; He will do what is just and right in the land. In those days Judah will be saved and Jerusalem will live in safety. This is the name by which it will be called: The Lord Our Righteous Savior."

Jeremiah 33:14–16

Alright, since we are becoming friends, I would like to tell you a little bit more about myself in my younger years. I lived with my mom, dad, and two sisters in a sweet little suburban home. Yes, I was blessed with many people in my home and in my life, but the reality of my story is I was disappointed quite often with promises that were not fulfilled. This may come as a shock, but the words "I promise" are not easy words for me to hear or say. It wasn't until I read this passage the Lord spoke through Jeremiah that I was comforted. It was hard for me to understand how a Father who I can only hear and not physically see could make a promise and keep it. Let's put a pin in this conversation, and we will circle back to my story in a bit.

31

The Lord gave a promise to His people so they could cling to a hope and be joyful while waiting. Oftentimes we forget God is God, not man. (See Numbers 23:19.) Man has distorted our way of thinking. And if you do not agree, you have the best head on your shoulders, and I would love to talk with you. However, from where I am and what I have endured, people have made promises and not fulfilled them. Can you relate?

We are people who want people to follow through with their promises.In this particular scripture, we see God extending His promises, which refer to both the first and second coming of Christ Jesus. In the first coming, He would be born of a virgin and die in order to save His people from their sins and iniquities. In the second coming, He will also come to save His people, but this time to execute justice and righteousness throughout all the earth.

Now, let's take a venture to the good book of Isaiah. God said He will make a righteous Branch sprout from David's line. (See in Isaiah 11:1; Jeremiah 23:5.) The Branch talked about is the Word in the flesh, Jesus. This is the story of the Christmas tree from Day 3 all over again. Follow me on this one as I am connecting some dots for you. When someone speaks, they use words, correct? So what makes it any different when God speaks? Each word we read in Scripture is in fact God-breathed. (See 2 Timothy 3:16.) So why do we question Him when He speaks to us now, when we do not question the words He spoke in Genesis during the six days of creation? Well, for me, I falter in the way of thinking because as mentioned before man distorts the way we think.

Alright, let's pull the pin and talk about some reasons why it is hard for me to believe promises. We left off on the subject of the dynamics of my family. I had been let down by people's promises, and I'll be honest with you, I was not a joyful person. Have you ever been in a similar phase in your journey?

Have I told you the story about the time I got a pony? If I haven't, here we go. My dad and I were heading out to this sweet little farm tucked away in the plains of Mississippi. I was eager and excited to meet my first pony. I thought about how my cousins raced and rode their horses, so I started dreaming of how I could potentially do the same one day. So I started asking my dad a million questions about horses. And as we drove up, I saw off at a distance this beautiful white pony. He was standing off by himself eating the grass and enjoying the day. Instantly I jumped out of the truck, headed toward the gate, and then stood still in awe and disbelief that this little pony was all mine. I just knew it had been mine; without asking or someone telling me, I knew he was mine. As I learned more about my new little friend, my mind was flooded with all the possibilities and adventures we two could have.

On the way home, I remember the smile on my dad's face. He was excited for me! He made a promise to me that we would come see my little pony once a week. And not a moment too soon, this hope-filled promise took a turn. The sweet little pony I had dreamt of doing adventures with was stripped from me. I don't think my dad intended on not being able to stand firm to his promise, but he let me down. Once again, I felt the opposite of love. How could my dad not live up to his promises? He is my dad. He is supposed to provide for me joy, peace, and abundance in life.

It was not until I began a relationship with Jesus that I realized my earthly father is not my Heavenly Father. And the promises God makes, He will fulfill, and the promises man makes, cannot all the time. And as I began the journey, I started to read about promises God had made to His creation.

Lovely Encouragement:

There are over 8,000 promises written in the Bible spoken by God!

The spoken promises started in the garden of Eden. Adam and Eve walked with their Father in the most perfect place. And, of course, when reading this, my mind was flooded with memories of me walking through life alongside my dad. Truthfully, it did not look anything like the life Adam and Eve had with their Father. Then all of a sudden, they too began to listen to someone else's promises, other than their Heavenly Father. Therefore, they doubted the promises of their Dad.

God not only made promises to Adam, Isaiah, and Jeremiah but also to you and me. The "Courtney definition" of the word *promise* means you do what you say you are going to do.

Lovely Encouragement:

It was not an overnight process for the promise God gave Jeremiah to be fulfilled. The timeline from Jeremiah to Jesus was about 600 years.

And due to there being a waiting time of praying while you wait, I want to shed some light and send you some encouragement during your journey. I did not want to be sad or disappointed by my earthly father; he did the best he could do. Yet the reality is, I was. Because again, my earthly father was not my Heavenly Father. So I did what Jeremiah did. I clung to the promise spoken by my Father.

In the same way that God gave promises to these men and me, I have some questions for you. When you answer them, I encourage you to take them to the Lord in prayer and allow Him to help you in a loving way as you wait for your Heavenly Father to fulfill His promise(s).

Questions

» What promise(s) has God given to you?

» What are the verses you hold onto while you wait for the promise(s) to be fulfilled?

» Are you allowing those verses to help you focus on Jesus and not on the situation at hand?

» If a young woman of faith came to you years from now, what advice would you give her?

» Do you wrestle with God while you wait for these promises to be fulfilled?

Day 5

Praying for a Gift

In the time of Herod king of Judea there was a priest named Zechariah, who belonged to the priestly division of Abijah; his wife Elizabeth was also a descendant of Aaron. Both of them were righteous in the sight of God, observing all the Lord's commands and decrees blamelessly. But they were childless because Elizabeth was not able to conceive, and they were both very old. Once when Zechariah's division was on duty and he was serving as priest before God, he was chosen by lot, according to the custom of the priesthood, to go into the temple of the Lord and burn incense. And when the time for the burning of incense came, all the assembled worshipers were praying outside.

Luke 1:5–10

I will not lie. At first, when I read this passage, I thought to myself, *How can this scripture relate to Christmas?* I knew it related to Jesus because Zechariah and Elizabeth were Jesus' uncle and aunt, but I could not understand how it could relate to Christmas. And then the Holy Spirit gave me some insight, and that lightbulb like the star on top of the tree lit up in my mind. John the Baptist was a gift to Zechariah and Elizabeth (Elisabeth), and they had no idea!

37

Have you ever prayed or wished for one gift around Christmastime, but you did not believe you would ever get it? Maybe it was for peace and quiet, a clean home, new shoes, a fishing rod, a vacuum cleaner, dwarfs to come in and help around the house, or maybe just a mind that was at rest. Well, we see tucked in this passage a gift that is desired by many. This particular gift was one that was prayed for and waited on before the unexpected would happen.

Story time! Early one morning, a man wakes up next to his wife. They say a prayer together. And in this prayer, their soft, sweet voices talk to their Creator. More than likely tucked away in this prayer, they both expressed their deepest desire. Then the man cleaned up and got ready to leave as the man kissed his God-fearing wife and may have said, "Goodbye, I love you. And when I get home, I will help with the dishes, and we can talk about our day." And he heads out the door for another day doing the duties of husband, worker, and prayer warrior. He leaves with the intent of having an ordinary day. He may have shown up to work with his work friends, talked about the dinner they ate the night before, cast some jokes, and began the tasks for the day. So Zechariah and Elizabeth's story may not have gone exactly that way, but I like to imagine.

Even though I don't know the full story of this power couple, I do know some facts that will help us during this time of the holiday season. As we read in Luke 1, Zechariah was married to Elizabeth, and they were both righteous in the sight of God. Woah! That is a pretty big deal to be righteous in the sight of God. Zechariah and Elizabeth did not merely go through the emotions or motions of following God's laws;

they lived their lives with full integrity of obeying God's laws. Wouldn't you like to be like that righteous power couple?

During these days, there were about 20,000 priests divided into groups throughout the country, just as David instructed. Zechariah belonged to the division of Abijah. And there was a man named Herod, King Herod the Great. Being half-Jew, he would help the Jews, but only for political pleasure, not because he cared about their God. Now the story begins to unfold a bit more. Zechariah left home and began his normal duties at work, nothing special. Until the lots were rolled and God showed an ordinary family what extraordinary purpose He had in their lives!

Each morning a priest would enter the Holy Place in the temple and burn incense. Yet, before the priest could enter and pray, they would cast lots to see which priest would enter. On that day, the lot fell on Zechariah. This moment was not by chance; it was by plan. God's perfect plan! I am sure Zechariah's heart leapt when his mind caught up with what his eyes were seeing. Mine would have too. He knew this was an opportunity to go into the temple and pray to God. You see before Jesus came into the world, died for us all, and gave us an all-access pass to God, man used to have to meet with God in a building at specific times and on specific days. And that might be hard for you and I to comprehend because we are accustomed to praying anytime and anywhere. And if that doesn't give us some encouragement look at it from this angle. You and I can access God whenever and wherever because you are now the temple. (See 1 Corinthians 3:16–17.)

And now we see Zechariah in the temple (building) praying to God. What Zechariah did not know was that God would hear his prayer and answer it by giving him a gift. A good gift that he and his wife had prayed for, probably earlier that morning.

Before we can read and learn about his son all grown up who lived in the wilderness and who pointed everything back to Jesus, let's talk about the people and their backstories. Luke makes it a point to let us in on the secret to their marriage. Both Zechariah and Elizabeth congratulate God for everything. They were not young whippersnappers like Mary. Luke wrote that Elizabeth was not able to conceive, and both she and Zechariah were very old. (See Luke 1:7.) Do you remember the story of Abram and Sarah? God gave them a promise that through their son, He would establish His covenant with him as an everlasting covenant for his descendants after him. (See Genesis 17.)

Here stands Zachariah at the entrance of the temple, ready to embark on an intimate moment with God. He has an opportunity to pray and ask God for anything, and what does he do? Well, it may surprise some of us what he says. I cannot tell you exactly what Zechariah prayed for in the Holy Place because I have not researched it yet. Oh, wait! Yes, I can! It was a son.

Zechariah was chosen to go into the Holy Place and burn incense. (See Exodus 25 and 30.) Now, you are probably wondering what incense is and the best and simple way to describe it to you is that is a smoke of a sacrifice being burnt. And at that time, they did it twice a daily. So when the people saw smoke (the incense burning) they would pray as well.

It was a custom that when you saw smoke coming from the temple, you had an opportunity from wherever you were to stop and pray as well. At this time I want to stop where we are and have a "Zechariah moment." Right where you are today you have burdens you can no longer bear. And that goes the same for me. You feel bogged down and you might even feel beaten by them. So, instead of waiting to go to church to tell someone, I challenge you right here, right now, text someone and say, "I have a burden and I need prayer. Will you pray with me?" Chances are your friend you are messaging has a burden too, so let's send our prayers up like the smoke we are reading about and pray for our friends. For they believed that the smoke was a symbolic representation of prayers ascending to God on His throne. So, just as Zechariah was praying, so were the people. So, let your people do the same for and with you!

Lovely Encouragement:

Your burdens and your prayers are like the smoke of the incense can reach God (See Revelation 8:4 and Matthew 18:19).

Do you remember my question from earlier? Just for a moment, reflect on the time you prayed for a gift you truly desired, and you did not believe it would come to be in your possession. Since God can make a barren woman bear a son, give Abraham a promise and keep it, part the waters for His people to walk in freedom, send quail and manna from heaven, provide light in a desert, allow an entire wall to fall down in Jericho with a shout, make the sun, moon, and stars stand still, allow a widow to be a part of the lineage of Christ, allow Daniel not to be swallowed by hungry lions, and Jonah not to be swallowed by a large fish to then be placed back on the mission, why would you ever let the adversary say God cannot give you extraordinary gifts in your life? These were all ordinary people, living ordinary lives, in an ordinary day and time. Until their desire to obey drove them and their obedience to blessings.

Lovely Encouragement:

It is obedience that leads to blessings.

Can you imagine a life with no blessings or a Christmas with no gifts? Now, obviously, Christmas is not about the gifts. It's about Jesus and His presence being the greatest gift of all, and I come into your life as a close second! Zechariah had no idea the gift God was preparing was already being prepared through his and his wife's prayer.

Stay plugged in, friend, because tomorrow we are going to talk about prayer and how we ought to take care of our special gifts.

Lovely Encouragement:

I urge you, go pray that prayer! Go send your prayers up to our Father and wait expectantly and accept it when it comes!

Even if you have to pray for days, months, or even years, keep praying. And if you need people to come alongside you while you pray, reach out. Let us join together in prayer and send our prayers up to Father, God Almighty. Because I can assure you if Zechariah had not have prayed that prayer, he would have missed out on being a part of God's bless-filled story.

Questions

» If God were to answer only one prayer for you today, what would it be?

» When you go into your prayer time, do you imagine your prayers going up and the blessings coming down?

» What is your prayer life like?

Day 6

Cherish Your Precious Gift

Then an angel of the Lord appeared to him, standing at the right side of the altar of incense. When Zechariah saw him, he was startled and was gripped with fear. But the angel said to him: "Do not be afraid, Zechariah; your prayer has been heard. Your wife Elizabeth will bear you a son, and you are to call him John. He will be a joy and delight to you, and many will rejoice because of his birth, for he will be great in the sight of the Lord. He is never to take wine or other fermented drink, and he will be filled with the Holy Spirit even before he is born. He will bring back many of the people of Israel to the Lord their God. And he will go on before the Lord, in the spirit and power of Elijah, to turn the hearts of the parents to their children and the disobedient to the wisdom of the righteous—to make ready a people prepared for the Lord."

Luke 1:11–17

My oh my, glory, glory, glory oh my! I still get swept off my feet by God. Not only because of who He is but also He hears us and answers our desires according to His good and perfect will. (See Romans 12:2.) I can only imagine what Zechariah felt standing at the altar after praying to God a specific prayer.

Have you ever prayed a prayer so special and specific that when God answered it, you were in shock and awe all at the same time? I can recall the exact moment when I agreed upon a prayer of which I could not pray for myself. My heart was heavy, and my burden was great. I remember the place and moment and thinking back on it brings joy to my heart and soul.

I sat in my kitchen at my new home across the table from my discipleship leader. You see, I was beginning to experience God in a whole new way. Yet I was living a lukewarm lifestyle, and it brought me to tears. I cried, more like I wept. You know, that gut-wrenching cry that we have now deemed "the ugly cry." Yes, that was me experiencing the Holy Spirit and realizing I had been grieving Him for years now. The life I was living was not glorifying God or His temple (my body), and each day was worse than the last. So, I asked her what to do, and she began to pour Truth into me. It was then, I was able to shift my focus to the Lord and see my situation through His eyes. Metaphorically speaking, I gained the lenses of the Lord, and I received twenty-twenty vision on the situation.

As she shared what I should do, I wept louder and harder. At that moment, I knew what had to be done. And then I said what I never thought I would ever say, "I need to be out of my worldly relationship and begin a Wordly one. How do I break up with this man I want to marry?" And she said, "You pray." Such a short, sweet and simple answer. At that answer I began to weep uncontrollably not only because I was aware that I was going to have to end this relationship with the man I wanted to marry. I was going to have to surrender all the hopes, dreams, desires, and happiness that would come from our future together. She took me by my hands and began to pray on my behalf. I cannot recall what she prayed exactly because I was filled with many emotions, but I do know she prayed to God that He would allow him to break up with me!

Remember, my plan was to marry this man, build a life with him. We wanted to have children together, live out our dreams together, and do some churchy things when it was convenient for us.

Lovely Encouragement:

Any man pursuing your heart needs to already be pursuing God's heart. And the same for you. If you are going to pursue a man's heart, you need to already be pursuing God's.

Well, just like our story from today, Zechariah prayed on behalf of his best friend, Elizabeth. My leader did the same for me. God heard my friend's prayer, and He saw into my hurting heart and healed it by giving me His gift of joy in the midst of sorrow. I expected God to answer my prayer. However, the way He did it was unexpected. The very next day at noon, my prayer was answered. And what a relief it was for my Spirit, mind, and body! From that one moment, I began to see the power in praying.

As Zechariah stood at the altar and the angel appeared to him, I am sure he knew God was about to do something incredible. In the same way, when I sat across the table from my dear friend, I knew God was going to do something incredible, not only in my life but also in my boyfriend's life. You see, it is not that I did not love him because I did and I still do. However, the life we thought we wanted was not one that God would have looked on as righteous. We needed to let go of what we desired and shift our focus from the normal days and begin looking at what God was rolling in our favor. In the same way God did it for Zechariah and myself, He will do it for you!

Alright, back to the story. As Zechariah stood face-to-face with an angel of the Lord who gave Zechariah a promise from God. "Your wife Elizabeth will bear you a son, and you are to call him John" (vs. 13). He knew God had heard his prayers. Think about that for a moment; little did Zechariah or Elizabeth know at this time why God had not answered their prayer, *yet..*

John would be:

1. A *joy*

2. A delight to him

3. Great in the sight of the Lord

4. Filled with the Holy Spirit before he was even born.

The name John means, "The Lord is gracious."

God was gracious to me, and I would not trade those two and a half years and that one month for anything. Yes, in that moment of tears and heartbreak, I felt alone and unloved in the midst of the transition, but that was when God stepped in. I was ripe and ready, and God knew it. I guess you can say, He chopped away some things. After what I thought was my everything had been taken away from me, my prayer became, "Abba, I need *You*!" He heard me, stepped in, and saved the day and me! He had been there the whole time waiting for me to surrender. And finally, even though it hurt, I did. Now, the journey much like Zechariah was not an overnight experience. It took some preparation and prayer to be able to comprehend and be comfortable with the experience and the separation. And I want to encourage you in this way—*It is okay to pray for big things! It is okay to not be okay! And it is okay to not fully comprehend what is happening right in front of you!*

After the reassurance from God Almighty, Zechariah was promised joy would enter into his life. And it did! God loves to prepare His children for what He is preparing for them.

Lovely encouragement:

Be joyful with the sweet, small bundles, and when the blessings of the big prayers come, we will be overflowing with joy!

Prayer: Abba Father, thank You for being present even when I cannot feel You. I know You are a God who is holy, and You desire the same for us. Thank You for showing and leading by example how to be holy and live a life of honor. I will admit it is hard being holy. My evil desires entice me to go against Your instructions. Thank You for blessing me with Your written instructions and also for them. They help me stay close to You. Your words have saved me from many moments of despair and heartbreak. I love You, Dad. Thank You for loving me in the midst of my breakdowns and blessing me with Your abundant life! I pray these heartfelt words in the name of my best friend and Your Son, Jesus, amen!

Questions

» What areas of your life have you experienced God answering your prayers? (List them all.)

» What did you cling to in times of losing hope?

» Verses I clung to in my moments of preparation: "But those who hope in the Lord will renew their strength.

» They will soar on wings like eagles; they will run and not grow weary, they will walk and not be faint" (Isaiah 40:31), "Therefore I tell you, whatever you ask for in prayer, believe that you have received it, and it will be yours" (Mark 11:24), "The righteous cry out, and the Lord hears them; He delivers them from all their troubles" (Psalm 34:17).

» What are some of the promises God has given to man?

» What are the promises God has given to you?

» How are you holding tight to His promises?

» Are you willing to praise Him in the times of preparation?

» Dig deep here: How is God preparing you?

» Challenge: Take your prayers and write them down. Stick those prayers to your walls, doors, headboards, kitchen counters, dashboards, etc. This way, you can be reminded to keep praying. And as you see them being answered, write them as praises!

DAY 7

BE SILENT WHEN GOD SPEAKS

Zechariah asked the angel, "How can I be sure of this? I am an old man and my wife is well along in years." The angel said to him, "I am Gabriel. I stand in the presence of God, and I have been sent to speak to you and to tell you this good news. And now you will be silent and not able to speak until the day this happens, because you did not believe my words, which will come true at their appointed time." Meanwhile, the people were waiting for Zechariah and wondering why he stayed so long in the temple. When he came out, he could not speak to them. They realized he had seen a vision in the temple, for he kept making signs to them but remained unable to speak. When his time of service was completed, he returned home. After this his wife Elizabeth became pregnant and for five months remained in seclusion. "The Lord has done this for me," she said. "In these days He has shown His favor and taken away my disgrace among the people."

Luke 1:18–25

Yesterday we talked about waiting for our prayers to be answered. Do you find it easier and more exciting to wait for the gift (promise) from God now that you have some verses to cling to on this journey? As we approach today's reading, I encourage you to find yourself in a still place leaning into the Word and applying God's story from my life to yours during this season of life.

Zechariah is found in the same spot where we left him in yesterday's reading, standing in the temple, speechless. And just like us, sometimes we are found standing in the same spot, waiting and speechless. Zechariah had been promised a long-awaited prayer which was finally being answered. Yet, he may not have moved physically, his heart did spiritually. Zechariah is standing face-to-face with Gabriel as he presents a promise from God. And sweet Zechariah's heart doubts.

I remember reading this story and thinking, how could you not believe the voice of God. And then I was reminded of Abraham and Sarah's story and then my very own. At first glance, Zechariah had a simple question, "How can I be sure of this?"

Lovely Encouragement:

Zechariah's strengths and weaknesses:

Strengths:

> Righteous man
> Priest
> Fathered John the Baptist

Weakness:

> Doubted God's ability

Communication is a way of life. And during the Christmas season, conversations and questions overflow due to the emotions we have endured all year long. As we sit around the table, we love talking about the great adventures we have faced the last few months. However, for Zechariah, due to his lack of faith, God removed his ability to communicate. Not only was he not able to tell others what he experienced, but he was also not able to tell others what God was going to do.

Now you may think it was harsh for God to remove a man's ability to talk. Yet, that is our finite mind's way of thinking. What would have happened if Zechariah went on speaking of what God was going to do? It may have gone the way many of our conversations with God go. He may have exasperated the promise or withheld the moment of his heart doubting. Yet, God knew what would help him believe.

I am not sure of your story or if you have ever doubted God, but here is mine. God met me where I was, alone in a second-story apartment. I had just been let go from my job, broken up by my boyfriend, and had no direction for my life. There I was, lying on the floor, sobbing, and broken. You may be able to see into that sentence and completely relate to your own story of brokenness. And if you are able to go a bit further in the sentence and see the story, you will see my prayers were being sent up like the smoke in the temple. Yet they were not normal prayers, they were silent prayers. I had prayed to God and told Him everything, from my greatest fears to my deepest desires. In those moments, I doubted God was listening to me or even if He cared. How could He have allowed my precious dreams to be taken away from me and left me with nothing to hold on to for the future. I may not have been a weeping prophet at that moment, but I sure was a weeping woman. Not only had I allowed God to take everything, but I also gave myself permission to give it all to Him. I had forfeited everything, and for what? To be alone with no future, no income, and soon no place to live.

And just as the very last ounce of myself was surrendered, God began speaking to me. I knew it was Him because there was no one else in the room. At that moment, He gave me many promises. And unlike Zechariah, I did not doubt His words, well, at least not at first.

Lovely Encouragement:

As soon as I gave Him all of me, He gave me His word (promises).

Have you ever heard, "Relationships are give and take"? If you have, you may know where I am going with this. In the same way God took Zechariah's voice, God took my job, finances, future, and myself with the intent of blessing us more abundantly. You see, it was not a punishment but a privilege. Neither one of us knew in those moments why we could not speak, but it was clear God was speaking, and we needed to listen.

How do you think that conversation between Zechariah and an angel of the Lord went in the temple? Truthfully, it is hard for us to fathom how that conversation may have gone, but we are able to see what happens when you doubt God's Word. God may not take your speech like He did Zechariah, but He may remove something that is hindering you from fully believing what He is capable of doing with His power through you.

Lovely Encouragement:

Zechariah did not doubt what God could do, but rather doubted that God would fulfill such a promise through him. Believe and be silent when God is speaking.

Sometimes we do not take God at His word (promises) at first. It might be because the promise seems too monumental for us to achieve, or it might be because we do not see ourselves as qualified to help God with what He is doing. As Zechariah stood there speechless in front of his friends at work and then his wife at home, there was no way he could deny the fact that God was behind all that was taken away from him. Although he could not speak, I am sure he remained hopeful of the good news.

Perhaps the times we should hold tightest to the truth are in our moments of doubt. I know of a sweet, humble young woman who knew the Word so well that when the same angel of the Lord appeared to her, she too asked a question and then became silent. We will learn more about her journey tomorrow.

Are you in a season of faith-building in your life? If so, please be encouraged to not be shocked or doubt when God begins shifting or removing things from your life. You may lose something, but your faith will be increased! When you have the smallest amount of faith, it actually proves you do believe God can answer all prayers, big or small. (See Matthew 17:20.) Even those life-changing, life-altering, heart-wrenching, gut-churning, head-pounding prayers.

Lovely Encouragement:

Pray big and bold prayers!

Zechariah and his wife prayed for years to have a son. And many, many, many years later, God answered that one specific prayer. Why? Because God knew the right time to create and form John in his mother's womb. I am not saying that if he had been born one year earlier, the impact he had would have changed the world, but because he walked steps ahead of Jesus and proclaimed that the Messiah *is* coming, people did not have to wait too much longer for their prayers to be answered too!

Lovely Encouragement:

The best is yet to come. They started looking and waiting with patient endurance for the Messiah, their long awaited prayer, to come. Because John the Baptist was just a few months older shows:

1. No matter your age, you are still found not worthy enough to untie the sandals of the Messiah.

2. No matter what you think your ability is, you can do great things for the Kingdom and with God!

3. Your prayers are heard even when you are in the wilderness with *nothing* left to give.

---

4. What you have is enough because Who you have inside of you is more than enough.

5. When you point to the Messiah, make sure you are including others to see who you are pointing to, so they can be in awe of His words and works as well.

Now back to the story. Zechariah is unable to speak, his wife is pregnant, and they have a promise of a gift of joy waiting for them. However, how could this be joyful to either of them? They trusted the Lord at His word that He would turn their disgrace and grief into a glorious moment. And He did!

Lovely Encouragement:

Talk to Him now! You don't have to wait until the prayer is answered, you can praise right now!

Questions

» Why do you think Zechariah was in the temple for so long?

» How do you think that conversation between Gabriel and Zechariah went in the temple?

» Do you ever think, *I know God is powerful, but this I am not sure He can fix or even handle?*

Day 8

Highly Favored

In the sixth month of Elizabeth's pregnancy, God sent the angel Gabriel to Nazareth, a town in Galilee, to a virgin pledged to be married to a man named Joseph, a descendant of David. The virgin's name was Mary. The angel went to her and said, "Greetings, you who are highly favored! The Lord is with you." Mary was greatly troubled at his words and wondered what kind of greeting this might be. But the angel said to her, "Do not be afraid, Mary; you have found favor with God. You will conceive and give birth to a son, and you are to call him Jesus. He will be great and will be called the Son of the Most High. The Lord God will give Him the throne of His father David, and He will reign over Jacob's descendants forever; His kingdom will never end." "How will this be," Mary asked the angel, "since I am a virgin?" The angel answered, "The Holy Spirit will come on you, and the power of the Most High will overshadow you. So the holy one to be born will be called the Son of God."

Luke 1:26–35

My, my, my glory, glory, glory, oh my! Now, many of us have looked at this story and thought, *Wow, an angel of the Lord appeared to Mary and told her everything!* But that is not the case here. Mary, young and engaged to a man, probably, like many of us, thought many times about her life, future, desires, and dreams. She probably sat on the living room floor with all her friends and planned out her life with Joseph. You know those typical gal pals nights with scrapbooks and ideas spread across the floor. Mary and her friends may have talked about the future she and Joseph would have. Their conversations may have flowed with how many children they could see her with, without stressing her out, and who were going to be her bridesmaids.

They may have played with each other's hair and talked about a fairytale future, no one expected Mary's life to be the one you and I know about today. Now, the dreamer in me wants to keep going with all the possibilities, but I can't. I have to stick to the truth. Mary was young and engaged, humble and serving, knowledgeable and dependable woman. Those are just a few qualities of God that this young woman obtained. And in one moment, she may have been dreaming and desiring a life with Joseph, and the next, she is being presented by an angel of God with a whole new plan.

Have you ever been in planning mode? Possibly a season in your thought when you thought you had your life planned out and thought you knew exactly which way the Lord was sending you until that "Mary moment," the moment when God stepped in and gave you a new desire, new direction, new destination for your life.

Lovely Encouragement:

It might be a life-altering, life-changing, soul-winning, heart-piercing for the kingdom of God because if it's not, then how can you align your desires with His?

Mary is found standing before the same angel of the Lord, Gabriel, that Zechariah had stood before months prior. Yet their hearts were not in the same posture. Mary asked the angel a question just like Zechariah. However, her question, "How will this be, since I am a virgin?"

Lovely Encouragement:

Mary's question was pointed from a place of knowing that it would be done, even though she did not know how it would be done.

It would have been easy for Mary to say no to Gabriel. She was well aware that she would be the first and the last person to ever carry the Messiah within her. And she was also aware that she would be taking a path no one had ever trekked before her or would ever trek. She took the great promise and allowed her life to be changed in order to greatly impact the world.

Lovely Encouragement:

Mary did what was important not only for the kingdom
but also for mankind.

Mary had no idea she would be the mother of God's Son and give birth to the Son of God and raise a sinless man moments prior. If you read on, you will see these words spoken by Mary to the angel, "For no word from God will ever fail. I am the Lord's servant, may your word to me be fulfilled" (Luke 1:37–38)

As you have been reading this beautiful devotional the Lord and I wrote for you, filled with joy, love, and adoration of God, you may have seen my love for Jesus as we have compared not only my story to the stories of old, but also how you can relate to these characters as their stories unfold.

Today we have learned more about Mary and saw how she might have felt the moment her life was changed for the better. I feel compelled to stop and address a pressing subject on the matter of Mary. As the Scriptures have shown us, Mary was in fact Jesus' mother, and she carried Jesus in her womb for the full term and then gave birth to Him. It is not possible to deny that fact. However, as sweet, humble, and courageous as Mary was to say yes to God, she did nothing for you or me. Well, other than carrying our Savior and caring for Him as He grew older. Even though Mary carried Jesus in her womb for full term, He was the one who carried the cross up a hill to bear her sins. And He did the same for you and me. I pray only to Jesus because Jesus is my Savior. It is through Him and His willingness to wear my sin and shame that I am saved.

> *Lovely Encouragement:*
>
> Mary was a simple gal who answered the call; Jesus is the one who bore the sins for us all.

There are many women in my life whom I call my "Elizabeths." These are the ladies who have held me accountable on the righteous path and helped me on this journey. There is one particular lady who comes to mind as I write about Mary. This woman resembles her closely, and if God would have waited until today to choose a mother to take care of His Son, I am sure this would be the lady for the job. Not only is she a devoted daughter of the King, but she is also a wife, mom, teacher, caregiver, photographer, choreographer, counselor, business owner, and even a prayer warrior. She has been one of the women I lean into when I see all the ingredients (responsibilities) in the kitchen and helps me formulate a recipe to help make sure I don't, unknowingly, break the plate.

Mary does the same for us throughout her journey. Throughout her story, she shows us who to say "yes" to when the responsibilities pile on our plates and why we ought to remain steadfast in the Word. The words may come directly from God or from His Word written years ago. Mary has taught us many things today, and one of those is how to say yes, even when we do not know the rest of the plan.

I want to encourage you, sweet friend, to keep a tight grip on the Word. Not only will it help you stay balanced in life, but you will also feel more confident to say yes when you hear the calling to embark on the journey as you follow joy through life. Now, I am sure Mary was scared to carry the Savior of the world, but to also be the first and last to do so. Saying yes to that calling must have been a fierce and faithful journey. I mean, come on, there was no social media to rely on or even a woman to lean on in times of uncertainty, but she leaned into God and those around her during the unknown. And you can too!

Lovely Encouragement:

Mary stands as the pioneer for God's people to say yes
as we walk through the unknown.

You may think there is no way you can help God! Oh, sweet friend, you most certainly can help God. He is not only a God who loves letting His children help in the garden (days) of our lives, He also delights in it.

Lovely Encouragement:

Do you ever think:

I am too old.

I am too young.

I don't know Scripture that well.

I don't know where to start.
I am not brave enough.

I am not equipped!

Now say:

I am the exact age I need to be to answer the call

from God.

I am taking the time to learn the Scriptures.

I am at a starting point now!

I am strong and courageous!

I now have equipment in my hands.

Questions

» What was the first sentence Mary heard from the angel of the Lord?

» Do you think God would say the same to you? Well, He does, He did! Write out these verses, please:

Isaiah 41:10: _____

_____

_____

_____

_____

_____

John 15:13: _____

_____

_____

_____

_____

_____

Psalm 17:8: _____

_____

_____

_____

_____

_____

Can you imagine if you went to the Lord right now and asked Him to begin to reveal His plan for your life? What do you think His response would be? Maybe something to the effect of, "I have great plans for you" or "My ways are higher than what you can imagine or think. Trust Me."

Have you ever had a moment like that with Him? If so, I am rejoicing right alongside you! If you haven't, please join me in a prayer to help you open your heart, hands, and head to the Lord God Almighty and His great plan for your life.

Are you willing to step out of your comfort zone and step into God's confidence and clothe yourself and begin preparing your heart, mind, body, and soul for all that God will/has called you to do?

I urge you to go into a prayer and conversation with the Lord right now. I wouldn't want you to wait another moment because He is waiting on you to do what He has called you to do! He may reveal to you pieces of information, the finish line, or just the next step. But I assure you, in whatever fashion He presents your life to you, He wants the best for you!

Prayer: Dear Abba, I know I am only a human, but You are within me, which means I can do great things in life. I am open to whatever You have planned for me. Graciously give me what it is I need for the next great thing You and I will do. I will admit, I am a bit hesitant because I don't know exactly what You have planned for me, but I trust You. Truthfully my hesitation comes from me wanting to control, and I need Your help as I go forward in our next great adventure. I adore You, Abba, and I am excited to do life with You, come what may. I pray this prayer from my heart and in Jesus' name.

Amen.

Day 9

Decisions, Decisions

This is how the birth of Jesus the Messiah came about: His mother Mary was pledged to be married to Joseph, but before they came together, she was found to be pregnant through the Holy Spirit. Because Joseph her husband was faithful to the law, and yet did not want to expose her to public disgrace, he had in mind to divorce her quietly. But after he had considered this, an angel of the Lord appeared to him in a dream and said, "Joseph son of David, do not be afraid to take Mary home as your wife, because what is conceived in her is from the Holy Spirit. She will give birth to a son, and you are to give him the name Jesus, because He will save His people from their sins."

Matthew 1:18–21

It is absolutely incredible that God, the Creator of all things, gives us the permission to make decisions. God grants us the ability to dream big dreams, wonder the "what-ifs," and make decisions based on our dreams. Yet, you and I know that we should venture back to the Divine Planner for whatever decision we are considering.

> *Lovely Encouragement:*
>
> The problem occurs when our decisions, desires, or dreams do not align with God's decisions, desires, or dreams.

Here we open the pages to a sweet love story between a man and a woman. This couple is pledged to be married and begin a new journey through life together. In yesterday's reading, we focused on Mary. We read about her bravery and her faith in God to say yes to a journey that neither she nor anyone had taken. As we have been venturing into the people and their stories as it pertains to this source of all love around the holiday season, we see the characteristics of God. We have not yet ventured into the life of Jesus and for obvious reasons, but I would like to take a moment and talk about his earthly father, Joseph. Not much is said in the Scriptures about this man of God. So, take a stroll with me as we talk about this man chosen by God to father His only Son.

Joseph was Jesus' earthly father while God is His Heavenly Father. (See Matthew 1:1–18.) Matthew sheds light on his lifestyle as a husband, father, and career man. Joseph is from the lineage of David. Therefore, he studied the law and was faithful to its teaching. We learn more about this man as we are shown his career path; he was a craftsman and worked skillfully with his hands. (See Matthew 13:55.) He was also a man of few words; actually, there is no record of him ever speaking a sentence in Scripture. Joseph shows us the action and faith it takes to walk in lockstep with God.

> ## *Lovely Encouragement:*
>
> God desires the best for us, and little did Mary and
> Joseph know they were chosen to be the parents of
> Jesus! Your family is the best for you. Whether you
> know it or accept it. Just as God chose Joseph and
> Mary to parent His Son, those in your life God has
> chosen with His best intention in mind.

Mary stood there face-to-face with the man she loved and
told him that she was pregnant with the Savior. She was more
than likely apprehensive as to how Joseph would react, not
to mention what her response would be to his reaction. Not
only was the child not his child, but it was not the traditional
pregnancy they had probably talked about for their future.

Due to the circumstances, Joseph devised a brilliant plan
to divorce Mary quietly and secretly. Now, you are probably
thinking the same thing I did. Why would he divorce her? Does
he not know she was chosen by God to bear His Son? Truth is,
we do not know. We weren't there for the painful, challenging,
life-changing conversation between the two.

> ## *Lovely Encouragement:*
>
> Due to the interruptions in our plans, we do what we
> do. We try to change the plans back or throw our hands
> up in the air and give up. All while God is putting His
> hands together and planning out our lives for us to
> prosper.

Now, let's talk about marriage. According to the Torah, there are steps to becoming husband and wife. I studied the Jewish customs about marriage, and I discovered some simple truths that will help us understand a bit more about the behind-the-scenes actions as to why Joseph was choosing to divorce Mary.

There was a process, and still are steps to be taken as it pertains to the marriage between a man and woman in the Jewish culture. The first step is betrothal (Hebrew *kiddushin*). And then following is when the man takes the woman home (Hebrew *nissu'in*). Thus the story of Joseph and Mary, right? No, this is where their story takes a ride off into the sunset, but with a different horse and into a different kind of love story. Their ultimate plan was that of their customs. But God had other plans.

It is not God's intent for a man to leave his wife due to the unpredictable move of God. In fact, Scripture says something quite the opposite for a man and a woman after marriage: "That is why a man leaves his father and mother and is united to his wife, and they become one flesh" (Genesis 2:24).

Has there ever been a time in your life when you made a decision due to the situation that was being presented to you? Of course you have. We all have. Everyday. All day long.

Alright, back to the story. Joseph lay down one evening; thoughts raced through his mind of what to do. He may have tossed and turned, hoping and yearning this wasn't his reality. He must have been thinking that Mary was unfaithful, and how could this have happened. And as he drifted off to sleep, God met Joseph where he was, in the midst of his thoughts. Joseph may have felt sorrowful, confused, and even heartbroken. Yet, in the midst of those emotions, God gave Joseph a hope in the present for a new love for the future. God sent an angel to Joseph in a dream to tell him what the next step was in the journey. That night God gave Joseph the rundown of His desire for mankind. It was at that moment Joseph was able to make a new decision based on God's desire.

Let me repeat: the problem occurs when our decisions, desires, or dreams do not align with God's decisions, desires, or dreams.

It could not have been easy for Joseph to walk side-by-side with his soon-to-be wife through a challenging journey of uncertainty. Yet, if we can learn anything from their story, we can learn that they trusted God. It would have been easy to say yes had they seen what all they would have to endure. However, God allows interruptions along our uncomfortable journey so we can find comfort in communicating with Him.

Lovely encouragement:

Through the journey,
love is with you every step of the way.
As we continue reading and leaning into the most
beautiful love story, stay plugged in here, friend.
Because tomorrow we are going to continue talking
about Joseph and learn from him how to have self-
control, sensitivity, and how to surrender.

Questions

» As our hearts have learned more about this beautiful, unpredictable love story between a faithful man and a favored woman, we saw there is no way man can ever produce true love, only God. What areas in your life are trying to produce joy?

» The trial, temptations, or situation that you are in right now, do you need to "sleep on it" or "surrender" it?

» What would your life look like if you continued "sleeping" through the situations? Truthfully, would your life look like a constant snoozefest?

» Do you need a wake-up call from the Lord? If yes, ask Him.

» If a young woman ten years from now approached you with a similar story that you are walking through at this moment, what would you say to her to help her through this journey? Maybe she does not necessarily want joy, but maybe she needs a hope to cling to. Would you be able to help her by the way you asked God for help?

DAY 10

DESIRES DEMAND DAILY DEVOTIONS

All this took place to fulfill what the Lord had said through the prophet: "The virgin will conceive and give birth to a son, and they will call him Immanuel" (which means "God with us"). [Isaiah 7:14.] When Joseph woke up, he did what the angel of the Lord had commanded him and took Mary home as his wife. But he did not consummate their marriage until she gave birth to a son. And he gave Him the name Jesus.

Matthew 1:22–25

When I read Scripture, I ask God to reveal to me through the Holy Spirit what I am reading so I can gain a better understanding of what was taking place during that time. I want to take a moment and talk to you about prophecy. Prophecy is simply hearing what the Lord is saying and sharing it with those around you. As we read today's Scripture we are in fact reading a prophecy being fulfilled. Truth is, when Isaiah spoke these prophetic words, they had no idea what "God with us" could possibly mean. Would there be a burning bush all the time? Would there be a cloud leading us every day of our lives? During this time it was probably hard for them to understand or even believe how God was going to be with them as they were in those dark days.

The moment Joseph woke up from this midnight, miraculous dream, he quickly changed his itinerary and followed suit with God's plan. He placed himself in a position to be a part of God's prophetic, perfect plan spoken through one of His people, Isaiah. This new jam-packed plan would be filled with fun, exciting, and unexpected adventures. And one of those unexpected adventures would include self-control.

After Joseph and Mary were married, they did what every couple does: they rode off into the sunset and lived happily ever after. Isn't that what happens? (Every woman ever married reading this just scoffed, smirked, and shook their heads.) Because just like the fairytale of them riding off and living a happy life is made up, too. Their first month, week, and even first moments as newlyweds were a shock. Not only were they going to be doing life together as husband and wife, but they were going to be leading, teaching, and correcting the Son of God. Just take the weight of that responsibility into perspective.

Besides, their first night as man and wife, Joseph teaches us how to be obedient to the Word of God. He did not act on what most would act upon when becoming man and wife; he showed self-control. I guess you could say, "Like father, like Son." Because this man of God stuck to his roots, self-control was one of the fruits that we see shoot. Take a look at this man's ability to say "no" in the face of earthly normalcy and say "yes" to desires of heavenly and holy ways.

As I was learning more about Joseph, I was reminded of the story when Jesus was led into the wilderness to be tempted, yet He walked out of the wilderness without acting upon any of the temptations or desires. Jesus was just as much man as Joseph, and He withstood the temptations because He had learned from

His earthly father self-control. Not to mention He was also God; therefore, He could not be tempted. (See James 1:13.) We do not know all of what happened in the wilderness as far as the temptations Jesus endured, but we see through His earthly father's actions along with learned behavior, He was able to have self-control over the temptations. (See Matthew 4:1–11.)

Lovely Encouragement:

We see both of these men's ability to resist the desires of what they know is normal and say "no" to what they know is right. Temptations will be in your journey; what you do with them or do not do with them shows your willingness to have self-control.

Joseph was a man who truly understood what it was like to live a holy life. I honestly have no idea what was running through Joseph's mind and out of his mouth as he kept tight to God's promises in one hand and held Mary in the other hand. But he showed us how to stay true to the Word of God. He did not consummate the marriage until Jesus was born. And by doing so was a true act of self-control. Especially for the man God chose to father His Son, Jesus.

Lovely Encouragement:

Mary was called to hold Jesus in her womb, while Joseph was called to hold her hand while holding the hand of God. Hold tight to the hands around you as you hold tight to the promises of God.

Sometimes I have a hard time controlling myself. Do you suffer from the same? Now, I know nothing can ever pluck me from my Father's hand, and I can never wreck God's ultimate plan. (See John 10:28.) Yet, my flesh (and by flesh I mean all the parts of my body) gets in the way of controlling myself and saying "no"more to earthly desires and saying yes to heavenly desires. Check out this passage written by Paul to warn us against temptations:

So I say, walk by the Spirit, and you will not gratify the desires of the flesh. For the flesh desires what is contrary to the Spirit, and the Spirit what is contrary to the flesh. They are in conflict with each other, so that you are not to do whatever you want. But if you are led by the Spirit, you are not under the law. The acts of the flesh are obvious: sexual immorality, impurity and debauchery; idolatry and witchcraft; hatred, discord, jealousy, fits of rage, selfish ambition, dissensions, factions and envy; drunkenness, orgies, and the like. I warn you, as I did before, that those who live like this will not inherit the kingdom of God. But the fruit of the Spirit is love, joy, peace, forbearance, kindness, goodness, faithfulness, gentleness and self-control. Against such things there is no law. Those who belong to Christ Jesus have crucified the flesh with its passions and desires.

Galatians 5:16–24

Truth be told, I care about what others think and say about me. And I will act on some of these temptations to stay with normalcy. I am being open and organic here with you, friend. There was a season in my life when I needed help, as we all do. So I reached out to a group of friends and explained what I had been going through and asked for help and prayers.

My story does not include bearing the Savior of the world, but it does resonate well with holding back from what the flesh desires. Through Joseph's life, we are taught not to be enticed by evil desires and withstand against the evil one in times of temptations. Night after night, Joseph lay next to Mary, his beautiful wife, and refrained from the act because he desired to be a part of God's promise. And for us, sometimes the days in and days out are challenging because we try so hard not to act on the very thing we desire, just like Joseph.

Lovely encouragement:

Joseph refrained from acting on what man desires and desired to act on God's way of reconciliation for man.

As mentioned before, I struggle with what others think of me. I am still learning to surrender it to the Lord. Night after night, day after day, as I think about what I will eat, say, and do, I lean into the hands of my Father as He guides me through this journey. He is lovingly providing me a way for me though the temptation (See 1 Corinthians 10:13). My realization did not happen from a midnight dream but more like a miraculous conversation. I sat down with my Father and told Him of my concerns, worries, and doubts. And then I asked Him what He thought of me. My Heavenly Father blessed me beyond what I could have ever imagined. He gave me guidelines and end goals for my life. It included food, faith, fitness, friendships, and family, and above all, a fearless prayer life. Joseph kept his motives in his heart, and so do I. And you can too, friend.

From our stories, I hope you see there is hope in listening to our Heavenly Father when you really do not know what to do or when you know what you want to do. It is hard to say "no" to what you really want. Trust me, I am in the same boat as you. It is a challenge, but we can do this together!

Questions

During this journey of following through this story of *love*, we have been given an opportunity of learning from the man who led Jesus. Joseph taught us to be silent in some situations, sleep while we wait for God to give us guidance, and today we are taught about Joseph's self-control according to God's plan.

We are going to go deep in today's questions, so If you need help with what to do or even what not to do, you can ask your Heavenly Father.

» Are there areas in your life where you are questioning if you are doing the right thing?

» Are any of those areas mentioned in Galatians 5:19–21? If yes, read on through Galatians 5 and check out what you are able to do when joyfully following Him through the journey.

» Too often, we are told what not to do. However, we are given what not to do to protect ourselves. It is righteous of you to seek God's way over what you think is the good way. And let me warn you, my dear friends, sometimes your own friends or family may consider what you do "wrong," but if you are following God and obeying what He has called you to do, you will do the "right" thing, even if others may say it is "wrong." Jesus was called a righteous Branch

because He did things the right way. Be like Him and
do what is right, even when the world says it is wrong.

Lovely Encouragement:

Walk by the Spirit. Be led by the Spirit. Live by the Spirit.

Day 11

Joy-Filled Visitation

At that time Mary got ready and hurried to a town in the hill country of Judea, where she entered Zechariah's home and greeted Elizabeth. When Elizabeth heard Mary's greeting, the baby leaped in her womb, and Elizabeth was filled with the Holy Spirit. In a loud voice she exclaimed: "Blessed are you among women, and blessed is the child you will bear! But why am I so favored, that the mother of my Lord should come to me? As soon as the sound of your greeting reached my ears, the baby in my womb leaped for joy. Blessed is she who has believed that the Lord would fulfill His promises to her!"

Luke 1:39–45

Have you ever been so excited about something that you took off running out of pure joy to tell your friend(s) good news?

Let me set the stage for you. This beautiful story takes place just days after Mary's encounter with an angel of the Lord. She had been blessed by God to carry the Messiah inside her womb all while helping fulfill the promises of the Lord. After pondering the words of the Lord, she could no longer contain all that He was about to do. She wanted to talk to someone about what was going on and seek wise counsel. This could have also

85

been due to Joseph protecting her from the people who knew her best. Because, after all, she was pregnant before she and Joseph were married, and he did not want her to be stoned, rebuked, or ridiculed.

We pick up in her story where she is found hurrying to tell her cousin Elizabeth about the good news. I am sure at this moment she is still overwhelmed with excitement, concern, or even perplexed. But nonetheless, the Lord has promised her and her husband, Joseph, that they would parent the Prince of Peace.

Can you imagine what emotions she was feeling and what thoughts were running through her mind? No, really think about it with me. She was greeted by an angel and given a promise that she was going to raise up the man who would save the world from the darkness. And she is possibly now realizing the level of responsibility she is about to have. She was accepting of it because she trusted the word of the Lord. And she was eager to tell anyone, at least anyone she could trust.

Lovely Encouragement:

Mary was going to raise up the man who would one day raise up from the dead, leaving our sins as good as dead. She was quick to praise Him, and we get to do the same!

Now Mary is seen hurrying from Nazareth to Hebron to the house of Zechariah to tell her cousins the good news. And truth be told, this is a much-needed time for a family reunion. By this time, Elizabeth was in her second trimester with her first child.

The very son that was promised to Zechariah back in the temple when he prayed. (See Luke 1:11–17.)

As Mary approached the house of Zechariah, she greeted them. Much like what we do today. Just the sound of sweet Mary's greeting, the child within Elizabeth's womb leapt with joy. Can you imagine what that moment felt like for Elizabeth? Oh, to be a fly on the wall at this exact moment. Hearing the screams, shrills, and sheer excitement from these two as they exchanged miraculous stories.

Just the other night, I went over to my friend's house to see her because she had been in Italy for about a month. Now she and her husband are those fancy people who have a doorbell that records your rings, actions, and such. Due to my sheer excitement, I started ringing the doorbell and hollering for her out of excitement to come and let me in! I was excited to not only see her but catch up on all that had happened in our lives over the last month. I am sure it was the same as Mary when she greeted Zechariah and Elizabeth. She approached their home not only knowing the good news but carrying it as well.

Verse to encourage you in your journey: "Rejoice with those who rejoice; mourn with those who mourn" (Romans 12:15).

Now, Elizabeth, after being greeted by her younger cousin, could have envied Mary due to her opportunity, but she didn't. She showed excitement! In fact, she matched Mary's excitement and began blessing her with words of encouragement through prayer:

Blessed are you among women, and blessed is the child you will bear! But why am I so favored, that the mother of my Lord should come to me? As soon as the sound of your greeting reached my ears, the baby in my womb leaped for joy. Blessed is she who has believed that the Lord would fulfill His promises to her!

Luke 1:42–45

I truly believe Elizabeth and Mary's faith had been strengthened when Mary walked into Elizabeth and Zechariah's home. Not only because she was visited by her cousin with good news, but also she had a visit from the Holy Spirit. Because not only does it happen, but she tells us it happened, "As soon as the sound of your greeting reached my ears, the baby in my womb leaped for joy" (vs. 44). The Spirit allowed Elizabeth to go beyond the emotion of happiness and experience pure genuine joy!

Lovely Encouragement:

The Spirit of the Lord visited Elizabeth and experienced joy internally and expressed it externally. You too can experience joy internally and express it externally. With a smile, greeting, hug, or listening ear.

Oftentimes we long for others to match our emotions about what is happening in our lives. It may be like Mary's story when she had an amazing encounter with an angel and was eager to share the excitement! Or it could be a story like Elizabeth's, where you find yourself being encouraged by someone else's experiences. Either way, if you are excited about what is happening in life, I encourage you to share it with someone. You may be blessed, or what you share may bless someone else.

As I sat across the room from my friend and we shared stories from the past month, we rejoiced with each other. In fact, we talked about this very book. We discussed the topics of this chapter and the correlations between Mary, Zechariah, the Holy Spirit, and much more. Can I encourage you to do the same with what you are learning, experiencing, and enjoying? Tell the body of Christ.

Oh! Before we end today's journey, I was reminded thatZechariah was still mute during the encounter between the two. Can you imagine what he may have been thinking during this exchange of experiences? So, with that being said, I would encourage you to continue telling others because you have no idea what encouragement they may need on their journey!

Mary ran to tell the good news!

Run with excitement and joy to share the miracles God has done and is doing in your life!

Elizabeth rejoiced with Mary!

Encourage one another in their joyous moments! Not only will you bless them; you, in turn, will be blessed!

Even if someone nearby is silent, still show excitement!

Those who cannot fully express themselves because they do not fully know how to will be encouraged by your excitement!

Questions

» What are some exciting things happening in your life?

» What exciting things has God done in your life?

» What exciting thing is God doing in your life?

» What exciting things are you waiting on God to do in your life?

» If there are no exciting things happening in your life, ask some of your friends what exciting things are happening in their lives! (Oh, and try to encourage them through blessings!)

» Who do you run to when God does good stuff in your life?

» Is that person someone who is trustworthy?

» How does he/she react when you share the good news?

» Do you thank God first before running and telling your friends of the good things He has done?

DAY 12

PRAYERS: PRAISING AND PROCLAIMING

And Mary said: "My soul glorifies the Lord and my spirit rejoices in God my Savior, for He has been mindful of the humble state of His servant. From now on all generations will call me blessed, for the Mighty One has done great things for me—holy is His name. His mercy extends to those who fear Him, from generation to generation. He has performed mighty deeds with His (outstretched and mighty) arm; He has scattered those who are proud in their inmost thoughts. He has brought down rulers from their thrones but has lifted up the humble. He has filled the hungry with good things but has sent the rich away empty. He has helped His servant Israel, remembering to be merciful to Abraham and his descendants forever, just as He promised our ancestors." Mary stayed with Elizabeth for about three months and then returned home.

Luke 1:46–56

We definitely have an advantage on this side of the bind of the Bible, would you agree? We are given opportunities to read people's prayers in the midst of problems and even their praises!

I don't know about you, but if I had a superpower, it would be time traveling. I would travel back in time and plop myself down in the places of those people who prayed and praised.

I'd start with the desert places where we find Job, Hagar, and David. Then I would venture into the home of Hannah and Sarah to hear their passionate prayers of their deepest desires. Could you imagine standing in their presence knowing how God was going to answer them yet still experiencing the pain and passion behind their prayers?

Too often, we forget that our God loves us. He knows exactly how our prayers will be answered before we even speak them. (See Matthew 6:8.) He stands in our midst to travel this journey with us, never leaving us in the midst of angst or agony. With each consonant and vowel, groan and grumble what we say, He hears. And our Father knows what is best for us and intends to give it to us. I can testify to Him answering my prayers in such a way that I could have never imagined, dreamt, or thought of. All according to His purpose and plan for my life. And I am sure you can say the same.

Take a look at Mary's prayer; she more than likely had not dreamt of bearing God's Son. Maybe a son, but not God's Son. Yet, she had confidence and trust in Elizabeth to praise and pray to Him out loud. She prayed and praised her Father with boldness out loud while her cousin was in the room. I absolutely have enjoyed learning about their beautiful relationship as cousins.

Let me ask you a hard question. When was the last time you prayed openly without asking for permission in front of your friends or family?

Follow me as I imitate Him: remember my story on Day 11 where I told you of my friend who welcomed me into her home while I praised God out loud? As women, we love to talk! Do you agree? Well, with every word we speak, we have two choices, we can either compliment or complain.

Who is God to you?

Praise Him for who He is.

In the name of Jesus, pray for perfection, healing, wisdom, authority, power, etc. in the place you are right now.

Invite Him into this current situation. Say this with me: I do not know what to do about this situation in my life. Let it be Your will done in this situation and every day of my life.

Let me see Your work in my life!

Give me Yourself, the bread of life, because You are who I need for today.

I receive the blessing of Your forgiveness, Jesus.

Questions

» Which prayer in the Bible is your go-to prayer?

» Why do you resonate with that prayer?

» Who would you like to go back and listen to while he/she prayed? Note it can be more than one.

» Let me ask you again, when was the last time you felt comfortable praying out loud in front of your friend(s)?

» What is holding you back from praying out loud in front of those who love you and those you love?

» What are your most pressing prayer requests?

» Who can you talk to about these prayer requests?

Do This!

Today I would like you to pray like Jesus. Now, I know there are many prayer requests you have in your life, and although there is no step-by-step prayer based on each circumstance that arises, we can pray the Word of God back to God just like Jesus. After all, He does tell us, "Pray like this...."

This, then, is how you should pray: "Our Father in heaven, hallowed be your name, your kingdom come, your will be done, on earth as it is in heaven. Give us today our daily bread. And forgive us our debts, as we also have forgiven our debtors. And lead us not into temptation, but deliver us from the evil one."

Matthew 6:9–13

___/___/_____

Dear Heavenly Father,
(Who is God to you.)

_____

_____

_____

_____

(Example: You are my strength, comforter, healer, provider, Father, etc.)

(Praise His name.)

_____

_____

_____

_____

(Example: You are to be honored and respected because You are holy.)

(Pray heaven down.)

_____
_____
_____
_____

(Example: In Your name, Jesus, I pray perfection, healing, wisdom, authority, power, etc. into this place.)
(Ask for His will to be done.)

_____
_____
_____
_____

(Example: In this current situation, I do not know what to do, reveal to me Your plan and will for my life and all of the saints.)
(Ask for it to be on earth as it is in heaven.)

_____
_____
_____
_____

(Example: Your perfection and glory are among us all. Let us see You at work.)
(Ask so you can receive.)

_____
_____
_____
_____

(Example: Give me You, the bread of life for what it is I need for today. Give me the strength I need for today to live humbly, walk justly, speak kindly, weep openly, rejoice unashamedly— is that a word?—care for my friends and family in a loving way, work hard at the job you gifted me, etc.)

(Receive forgiveness.)

_____

_____

_____

_____

(Example: I receive the blessing of Your forgiveness, Jesus. You took on all my sins so I can sit here today with a guilt-free life. I receive forgiveness.)

(Forgive others.)

_____

_____

_____

_____

(Example: As often as I sin, I am aware that others sin too. Help me to forgive others the way You forgave me [Luke 23:34].)

(Lead me away from the temptation.)

_____

_____

_____

_____

(Example: I am by no means perfect like You. I praise You for being the perfect Lamb who said "no" to temptation. Lead

me through the moments of temptation so I may follow You as my example and guide.)
(Keep me away from the evil one.)

_____

_____

_____

_____

(Example: Protect me, Father, from the evil one.)

Day 13

He Is with You on Your Journey

In those days Caesar Augustus issued a decree that a census should be taken of the entire Roman world. (This was the first census that took place while Quirinius was governor of Syria.) And everyone went to their own town to register. So Joseph also went up from the town of Nazareth in Galilee to Judea, to Bethlehem the town of David, because he belonged to the house and line of David. He went there to register with Mary, who was pledged to be married to him and was expecting a child.

Luke 2:1–5

Several things are unfolding here in this passage, and truthfully, it gets me excited. Not only do we see God working behind the scenes on behalf of those He loves, but He is physically on the move as well. All of this was done to fulfill what the Lord had spoken through the prophets.

Yesterday you were given the opportunity to pray. How did your prayer time go? I want to encourage you to know that when you pray, you are giving permission for God to move.

In today's reading, we are shown that Joseph and Mary are still following the rules. They take the journey to the town of David because, as Luke states, this is where Joseph and his family are supposed to go during the census. Before we go any further, allow me to give you a bit of insight as to what is taking place. A census is basically a way to calculate the population of a country. (See Numbers 1.)

Caesar Augustus was the Roman emperor at this time, and he was large and in charge. Maybe not physically, but he sure did think so mentally. Caesar may have been counting on the numbers to be high to either feed his pride or show off as his political status. Either way, Joseph and Mary were simply going there to register and pay taxes. Joseph, as well as the other Jews, had little to no say as to what was to take place in his hometown. Therefore, they would pack up their belongings and families and head to the place where they were born.

Fun fact: Jesus was born in Bethlehem but conceived in Nazareth.

Nazareth=Branch (See John 15:4–11).

Bethlehem=House of Bread (Hebrew) (See John 6:35).

Joseph and Mary took this trip out of obedience to their superiors. Yet, they were met with trials and tribulations along the way. Can you imagine being pregnant while traveling long distances either by foot or on the back of a donkey? I have not had children nor have I been pregnant, but I more than likely would not want to travel that in my single, non-pregnant life. I would like to send a text for this census this year, please! Yet, Mary did it willingly. In fact, both of them did, out of obedience.

And I am sure they were not even thinking about their obedience being blessed. Here Mary is about to give birth, and the last thing in her mind is probably taxes, trips, and a head count. And then you have Joseph, a man who is used to making stuff with his hand, a real thinker, and he is unable to fix this travel. But why does he do what he did? The theme of today's talk, obedience.

Lovely Encouragement:

Through the trials of traveling, God is faithful to fulfill His promises!

If you, at any moment in your life, have ever felt like you are walking a road that is filled with trials, temptations, and tribulations, I will break it to you like this because if I don't I am not sure any will. If you feel, think, or know you are on that road, your feet are on the righteous path. (See Psalm 1.)

And to add to that sure fact, you are in great company. The same enemy that we read about in Scripture is still alive. He is like a lion who prowls around, waiting to devour you on your journey. (See 1 Peter 5:8.)

But you have a Father who has already allowed Your brother and friend, Jesus, to take the path and cut down the vine (lies), cobwebs (sins), monsters (liars) for you. When it seems difficult, it does not mean God is distant. Let me repeat that for you in case you wanted to shut off on this one. When it seems difficult, it does not mean God is distant. He is in fact there with you; you just may be focused on the problem and not the Promise Keeper.

Mary was traveling a difficult journey. Her mind was probably racing with all the "what-ifs" the people face today. And the truth is, we do the same. We fill our minds with the devastations before they even arise. They traveled thirty-one hours by foot to get from Nazareth to Bethlehem. They may not

101

have known it then, but they were fulfilling the prophecy of the Lord. Check it out:

"But you, Bethlehem Ephrathah, though you are small among the clans of Judah, out of you will come for Me ne who will be ruler over Israel, whose origins are from old, from ancient times" (Micah 5:2).

Joseph and Mary may have seen this as a trial, loading a pregnant woman to go travel, but God was with them the entire time! Did you catch that, friend? God was with them. They were not alone on this journey, and neither are you!

It may seem as though you are alone in all the things you do in the day, but you are not alone at any part of the days. (See Deuteronomy 31:6). Yes, He is with you taking classes, working a full-time job, whether it is a paid position or not (hello, caregivers and mothers alike). He is with you, dreamer, activist, entrepreneur, boss babe. He is with you, gym junkie, writer, singer-songwriter, artist, film producer, astronomer, physical therapist, manager, doctor, nurse practitioner, aesthetician, baker, banker, nanny, world traveler, photographer, teacher, counselor, and coach. He is there with you, director, principal, marine biologist, golfer, gamer, sports enthusiast, telemarketer, maintenance worker, direct sales, and all the paths alike. He is omnipresent. As He was with Mary in the flesh, He is also with you.

Not only will you see His love in the invitations to be obedient to His calling, you will experience His love is in the invitation into intimacy. When it is just you and Him alone, walking the path. Yes, you might be a mom of four or a grandmother of one, you are still in need of having alone time with God in order to make it on this journey.

Switching gears here for a moment, follow me on this path. There is a Truth to prove to you that God was answering a prayer that had been prayers over 400 years prior to this. Did I say 400 years? Yep. Sure did.

From the book of Malachi to Matthew, even though it is just a simple page turn for you and me, it was a long-awaited time for the prayer and prophecy to be answered. For four hundred years, God did not speak directly to His people. Some of God's people continued speaking to God, while others continued to speak about the prophecies that would be fulfilled. God remained faithful to their prayers and prophecy even when He was not responding. *That shows that man can be dedicated.*

It was not until Mary married Joseph that, through the line of David, the promise of God that all of this would come to be was fulfilled.

In Micah 5:2, it says, "But you, Bethlehem Ephrathah, though you are small among the clans of Judah, out of you will come for Me one Who will be ruler over Israel, whose origins are from of old, from ancient times."

Do you see that? One of God's people prayed a prayer out loud, and it was answered years and years later. *That shows man must pray in one direction.* So, when you go into prayer on your path, try your best to pray out loud. Just try one, dear, just try one.

Lovely Encouragement:

One prayer a day can help you stay the way and not sway.

You may feel weird or strange, but God wants you to pray to Him. He gave you a voice, and He desires to hear it. This kind of life is called a relationship. Switching gears back to prayer. When you pray, you are connecting your heart to God's heart. It does not have to a formulated prayer. It can be short and simple, or it can be detailed and descriptive. The most impressive prayers you may ever hear are the most intimate prayers. The prayers prayed by Hannah and David were from places of sheer exposure because they were exposing themselves to the Lord.

My dear friend, I want to remind you of something before we wrap up today. You may seem small and unimportant sometimes, but that is 100 percent from the enemy. Who you have inside of you is a mighty, powerful, unlimited God!

Questions

» Have you and your Father talked about what He desires for you to do with Him on this journey?

» What holds you back from being obedient to God's calling on your life?

» If you don't have the calling yet, what do you enjoy doing that you could deem as you helping God?

» Truth is, God is not going to make you do anything you do not what to do. That is why you have to saddle up the donkey and ride to an unknown city. So, what is stopping you? Is it yourself, others, finances, degree, etc.?

» Dear friend, life is full of unexpected surprises! Are you up for the journey into the unknown? If you aren't, that is okay. Just learn to love where you are. If you are up for the challenge, get ready!

Day 14

Happy Birthday Jesus!

"While they were there, the time came for the baby to be born, and she gave birth to her firstborn, a son. She wrapped Him in cloths and placed Him in a manger, because there was no guest room available for them."

Luke 2:6–7

Fun fact: The mention of the manger is the basis for the traditional belief that Jesus was born in a stable. However, the stables that we see in nativity scenes are a close representation of the place Jesus would have His grand arrival. The stables that we speak of are actually spare rooms that are caves with feeding troughs (mangers) built or carved into the rock walls.

God's timing is perfect, wouldn't you agree? I went away to write this book one summer. In fact, I drove a total of eight hours to get away. I was under a great deal of stress, and I needed to get out of my mind and environment and get into writing this book. And let me tell you, I got out of my own way on this trip. My Heavenly Father and I had an incredible time together. He talked as I listened; He listened as I talked. I told Him of my desires, dreams, hopes, and needs. And along that eight-hour journey, He met every single one of my needs.

Little did I know that on my own journey to finding joy, I would be met with indescribable fear and disaster. However, in the midst of the journey, it would not occur to me that I would be changing today's devotion because God changed my plans. At the moment, I didn't feel this way but looking back, I sense and see His joy in the midst of my journey.

Let me walk you through my get-out-of-town story. I originally had requested the time off to go to a camp. Unfortunately, the plans for camp fell through, and I was going to have to work again that week. Yet, knowing the deadline of this editing process, God told me, "Go." I had no idea where I was supposed to go, but I guess I would know when I arrived. So fast forward to a week before my time off, I was giving God every excuse as to why I should not go, and He, in turn, would give me good reasons as to why I should go. And so I did. I packed up my boards, bike, and Bible and hit the road. I understand now why God told me "Go," but due to my inability to see His plan, I was near-sighted to the whole story.

Let me be the first to spoil the news for you. I do not do well with spontaneity; I enjoy plans. Yet, there I was, trusting God on that somewhat planned trip. Also, before I go any further because you might be wondering, I went by myself. I was not like Mary; I did not have a Joseph by my side. It started off kind of rocky, but after a while, I embraced the flow.

As I arrived at the beach, I was not only encouraged but also embraced by the sweetest and most supportive couple. Mind you, I traveled with the hopes of getting away from people, but I was met by God and His creation. I realized in that moment God was getting me out of my comfort zone and helping me to embrace new places and faces.

After a while, it was time for bed. Your somewhat-spontaneous friend did not make reservations anywhere. Uh-oh! Here I am searching for a place to stay. So I did what most young people do, I called my mom. At this point, I had already been driving for about five minutes in the pouring down rain, my windshield wiper had flown off, and water was seeping into my car where my board was strapped on top of my car. As I told my mom, "That's it! God told me to come here, and here I am with no place to sleep. I guess I will park at the most lit-up grocery store and sleep in my car." How could I have done that to myself? Planned-spontaneity? Sheesh!

I searched every hotel, motel, rentable home I could find on the web. I had my friends in Memphis and Ohio scouting out places for me to sleep. Finally, I grabbed the wheel with sheer rage and realized I had not told God that I needed help. We experienced this beautiful journey together, spent hours in His creation, and even ate His good food. So, I did what I do quite often, I cried. And then I talked to my Dad and said, "You knew I would be making this trip. In fact, You told me to come. Whether I misunderstood You or I went too soon, You knew I would be here. Can You help me find a place to sleep tonight other than my car?" At this point in the midst of this storm, a quite literal storm, I started to think that I doubted hearing my Father's voice. I did not have a moment like Mary where an angel appeared and gave me instructions for the next step. This was an audible voice, and I thought I misunderstood Him. So I began to apologize, and from there, the story takes a wild turn.

> ## Lovely Encouragement:
> A relationship between a Daddy and His daughter is knowing you can ask Him for help.

As soon as I talked to my Dad, my phone beeped with the message that read. "I have a place for you to stay." Yep, that is how my Dad works. My mom was on the phone with a friend, and she was gracious to let me stay with her. And get this, she lived thirty minutes from the place where I was getting my windshield wiper fixed and an hour from the beach I was at earlier. I truly believe God allowed my windshield wiper to break in order to get me closer to safety. I was not alone on this journey, but the enemy tried to convince me I was.

Lovely Encouragement:

Where God guides, God provides.

Now, back to the devotion. Mary and Joseph, although they may have thought they were alone, they were not. Mary had very little to give the King. In fact, all she could give Him were cloths. Can you imagine swaddling your sweet bundle of joy in cloths you had or rags you could find lying around just to keep your little one comfortable and warm? Yet, here she is, wrapping a King in rags.

Lovely Encouragement:

He will take the cloths (rags) you have and clothe you
in His righteousness.

Mary, with no mother's hand to hold while giving birth to the one the world would one day behold. While Joseph was by her side, not knowing what to do as Jesus cried. They were

110

blessed to hold the tiny hands of the one who one day everyone would scold. As she wrapped Him and held her Son close, she loved God more for saying "yes" to the life she chose. This young babe would not need ribbons and bows, for this child would one day be in crowns and robes. As she remembered blood falling on the floor, Mary held her baby, the one God chose for her to adore. She held Him tight, and with all her might, she remembered the screams that brought Him into the world through the day and well into the night. As Joseph knelt by her side, he humbled himself of all his pride. He knelt down and took Jesus in his arms and made a promise to God to keep Him from all harm. Jesus, as well as any babe could be, looked at His father and mother and thought, *Let it be.* As the angels were staring and saluting in their place from afar, God sent ahead a bright and glorious star. A star to be a sign of this promised King, who you would not find wrapped in bling.

There, the shepherds would find a babe wrapped in cloth lying in a feeding trough. And as they would appear, they would also hear the angels praising God in glorious song. However, for those whose hearts and homes denied the King would one day hear the slamming of their doors ring. It was not that they could not be opened again, but sooner rather than later was the hope for Elohim.

I have a painter friend who once painted a picture of Jesus ("Jesus' life"). And I hope it encourages you to keep your heart open to God and your homes opened to invitations. Yes, it is much harder to have people in your homes, but that does not mean you can't have people in your hearts. Continue to invite people into what God is doing in your life. Tomorrow we will see that God chooses those who seem too low to reach His glory. And yet He still reaches out His hand to pull into the fold all of those who deserve to know more about Him.

Lovely Encouragement:

I was looking for joy, turns out I was following joy through the journey.

Questions

» My story will look quite different than yours. You may not be told to go to the beach or across the borders, but where is God trying to take you?

» Will you be willing to stop and listen to Him? Not just when He says, "Go," but also when you feel emotional, alone, weary, etc.?

» Are you available to allow God to lead you past your comfort zone and into the unknown?

I will leave you with this small and simple yet inspiring word. The first sound to break God's silence was a cry.

DAY 15

GOOD NEWS OF GREAT JOY

And there were shepherds living out in the fields nearby, keeping watch over their flocks at night. An angel of the Lord appeared to them, and the glory of the Lord shone around them, and they were terrified. But the angel said to them, "Do not be afraid. I bring you good news that will cause great joy for all the people. Today in the town of David a Savior has been born to you; He is the Messiah, the Lord. This will be a sign to you: You will find a baby wrapped in cloths and lying in a manger."

Luke 2:8–12

Yesterday we were given an opportunity to celebrate alongside Mary and Joseph the birth of Jesus. Although it was a gruesome birth, it was a glorious one! The Savior had been born, and the first Facebook and Instagram posts were sent to some shepherds tending the flocks nearby. Well, not really. But there was a message about it as the angels took their post that night. Same thing, right?

In all honesty, can you imagine receiving *that* announcement? After waiting for years for the Messiah to come, the shepherds were the first to receive the invitation. That is exactly how these shepherds felt…well, aside from being terrified! The shepherds

were terrified, but their terror soon turned into joy! These
shepherds were not men from a palace or profitable men from
the land. In fact, they were poor men. They were the lowest of
the lows, and God ordained them, predestined them, to be the
first to receive the invitation to come and see the King.

Far off in the distance, the most unlikely crew of men were
performing their nightly duties. I am sure you have read of the
many times the angels were sent to deliver a message, and their
first response is, "Do not be afraid." And they say those words
not only because they are large and scary, but also because they
are not something you and I would normally see every day.

I hate to break it to you, friend, but angels are not the little
babies with arrows and cute little tushes you see in the church
bathroom. They are big and bright, with multiple wings and
multiple eyes. (See Isaiah 6:2; Ezekiel 10:12.) Which would
be part of the reason why the shepherds on that late night had
such a scare. Can you imagine working the night shift, and you
hear the familiar sound of those around you, and your eyes are
adjusting to the lack of light. Then out of nowhere, this bright
light appears and begins speaking to you? I won't lie, I would be
a bit startled as well.

As we shift gears for just a moment from the angels back to
the shepherds, I want to remind you that these shepherds were
the low end of the totem pole when it came to careers. Here
is a thought to ponder: maybe those shepherds were the ones
who supplied the lambs for the temple sacrifices or the ones who
performed the forgiveness of sins as it was according to their
custom. And here they are in a field and then invited to come
and see the Lamb of God who would one day be the ultimate
sacrifice for all sins, forever.

Lovely Encouragement:

God's heart delighted in those humble and low men in a field to come and see His Son who had just been born.

So, no matter if you think your job is insufficient, or you feel inadequate, or if you feel you need to climb the ladder of success, take a lesson from these men. I am sure they desired to be in a palace having grapes fed to them and leaves blown for a nice breeze, but had they gone the "rich route," they would have missed out on meeting the Righteous One. God most certainly did not choose the King to come see the newborn King but chose men whose hearts were humble and had it in their hearts to serve.

Questions

» Alone in a cave, Mary and Joseph held their son while God led men with humbled hearts to attend His Son's grand arrival. So my question to you is, are you humbling yourself to be a part of God's story or are you trying to write your own?

» So let me ask you, as much wealth as one can possibly obtain, would you have spent money to see the newborn King, or would you have wanted to be invited by God?

DAY 16

PEACE IS ON THE EARTH

"Suddenly a great company of the heavenly host appeared with the angel, praising God and saying, 'Glory to God in the highest heaven, and on earth peace to those on whom his favor rests.'"

Luke 2:13–14

We are arriving on the scene after the birth of Jesus as the angels were giving the grand announcement that peace has now come to the earth! Do you remember how we talked about God being silent for over four hundred years? Well, due to the silence, I believe He could no longer contain His emotions and excitement. So He sent a multitude of angels to go and announce the birth of His Son and sent forth angels to express His excitement.

To this day, I can remember walking through automatic sliding glass doors as I went to comfort and encourage my best friend as she was giving birth to her firstborn son. I had just left the funeral home for my grandfather, a place filled with loss and sadness. I had mixed emotions about the transition from celebrating a past life to celebrating a new life. Truthfully, I was dealing with conflicting emotions, yet I had a great deal of unexplained peace.

The angels had previously awaited in silence for the King to be born. Quite often, I look back on that day when my best friend was in another room while her friends and family were gathered in a waiting room anticipating the birth of her son. Those of us in that large room felt small at the time, but we were also feeling excited, joyful, and even peaceful. As we sat in silence, because we could tell something spectacular was about to happen, we heard the sound we had all been eager to hear—chimes. And then like a rehearsed dance, we all jumped up and cheered. The room was filled with chimes and then cheers. And that is exactly how I imagine it was when Jesus was born- cheering from God's creation. (See Luke 2:13–14.) All ten or so of us in that huge lobby at the hospital jumped up and hollered because we, like the angles, could no longer contain our own emotions. Not only that, the nurses and others in the waiting room cheered with us. Everyone was excited! We were not only joyful because of the new life in the world but also because of the great adventures we would have with him. Although there were no angels singing praises, the waiting room was filled with shouts of praise!

Many of us walk into a waiting room and find ourselves not wanting to rejoice because either the wait is taking too long or we aren't being encouraged during that time. Yet, if we turn the focus from us and ask someone who has been in a waiting room before, we can find comfort in the time of waiting. God waited over four hundred years to send His Son at just the right time. God made the promise back in the garden of Eden and waited years upon years before completing it. (See Genesis 3:15.)

Lovely Encouragement:

Your *waiting* time will be *rewarded* in time!

Questions

» What gets you excited about God?

» When you are in the waiting room, are you worried, or are you preparing to worship?

» Do you talk to God while you are in the waiting room?

» Try this, tell God right now your biggest worries while you are waiting.

» Do you believe that the waiting room is an unfair place to be? Why or why not?

Day 17

Be Where God Has Called You to Be

When the angels had left them and gone into heaven, the shepherds said to one another, "Let's go to Bethlehem and see this thing that has happened, which the Lord has told us about." So they hurried off and found Mary and Joseph, and the baby, who was lying in the manger. When they had seen him, they spread the word concerning what had been told them about this child, and all who heard it were amazed at what the shepherds said to them.

Luke 2:15–18

As I look over this passage, I can't help but see the obvious traits these shepherds have in comparison to Christians today. They were right where they were supposed to be in order to hear the proclamation of the birth of Jesus.

I typically wait to ask questions at the end, but I have a few for you to ponder on as we continue this journey. Have you ever had an encounter with God? One that you replay over and over in your head and desire to have again? Or have you had that deep, intimate moment with Him where you saw something, heard Him say something, or felt His presence? And immediately after, you wanted to run to the mountain top to tell everyone how good God is! Has that happened to you?

So often, when we hear good and exciting news, we flood people's feeds on social media and pour out what we saw. While that is not a bad thing, we can learn something from these men. First, they stood in amazement at what the angels of the Lord were saying. Secondly, they hurried to go see what the angels were talking about. Lastly, they ran and told of the good news.

> *Lovely Encouragement:*
>
> Run and tell people about how good God is!

Too often, as we desire for the bigger and better jobs in life, we miss the blessings that will take place when we are right where we need to be. Let's travel back to that open field where the shepherds are and take a seat there. I know we have been talking about these men for quite some time now, but they are a vital part in telling the story of Jesus. And I truly believe we can learn quite a bit from their part in telling His story. These lowly men more than likely desired to be in a palace as kings or working in the streets as merchants, but they did what they knew how to do.

Each step you take is the platform God has gifted you. You don't need the spotlight on you from the Hollywood screen or stage at church in the pulpit. Although that might be where you are or where you are headed, where you are right now is just as precedent for your purpose in life. You need to be where God needs you to be. You never know, you could be working in a field right now, shepherding the flock of many generations, and due to your willingness and obedience, you get to be part of receiving a blessing and then telling the good news of what God is doing to those around you.

Let's say God has chosen someone to be a teacher, and he/she is mentoring students while applying mercy, love, and grace throughout the week. What impact do you think the teacher is having on the students? Most would say quite a bit. But they would say that because they are remembering their teachers who impacted their lives. Yet in the teaching (sometimes called the trenches), the teacher may not see the blessing right away. It may take years before a student or students come back and give the teacher thanks for impacting their lives. The same was for the shepherds. They had no idea the impact they were having, but more than likely, they did not think they were making much of an impact where they were. But since they stayed right where God needed them to be, impacted lives through their teaching.

Those lowly shepherd boys were doing their due diligence as men in the field, tending their flock. Fun fact: pastors at church do this very thing each day they wake and walk. Just ponder on it. Their hearts were filled with great joy because they were where they were supposed to be.

Are you where you need to be? You might not be where you want to be, but are you where you need to be? And are you where God has called you to be? When I was on my "beach getaway," I knew God told me to go to the water. Truthfully, I had no clue as to why, but I went anyway. And come to find out, by me being where I needed to be, I had a marvelous time. It wasn't until the morning after the storm did I understand why God called me to the sea. One of the teachings I learned from my Teacher was to trust Him. He planned not only for me to meet young women who were going to help me find joy, learn to be fun again, and live life with planned spontaneity. And do you have any clue what else my Abba did for me that week? He allowed me to reconnect with family, run into lifelong friends, and meet new friends. Had I not gone on that "beach getaway," I would have missed out on many blessings. And those blessings have names, and all of them I dedicate this book to!

Questions

» Do you think you are working where God has called you to be?

» What area are you working in right now that you do not sense you are getting blessed?

» Would you trade the low life for the luxury life if that meant missing out on a blessing God designed just for you?

» Either way, God is going to bless you. But don't you want to have a big blessing versus a bite-sized blessing?

Advice for your journey:

Be present with the Lord—after all, He is the best present of all, and He gifted us with His presence!

1. Be willing to be humbled. Serve where He blesses you to serve.

2. Be aware. When He brings His glory into the fold of humanity, pay attention.

3. Be faithful. Go taste and see the promises He has fulfilled!

4. Be willing to run. *Go tell!*

Day 18

The First Mission Trip

"But Mary treasured up all these things and pondered them in her heart. The shepherds returned, glorifying and praising God for all the things they had heard and seen, which were just as they had been told."

Mary's obedience and love leap off the pages. She helps and teaches our hearts how to be in a peaceful place and ponder. As a woman with no kids, I can honestly say I do not know what I will do after I give birth. I may say only a few words, but then again, I may just be in such awe of the Lord and His miraculous works that I may be speechless (that'll be a shock).

Today we are reading about Mary, a humble woman of the Lord who said yes to God without knowing what it would actually entail. I often ask myself, "Why would she ponder and not wander about the towns telling of the miracle that just took place like the shepherds?" So many of us tend to flood our friends and family with the news, whether good or bad, to no end. I think that for many of us, the best way to get out what we have just experienced is through speaking about it or even posting about it.

For me personally, the way I process is completely different than the way my friends and family do. Yes, you and I are even going to process differently and that is because that is how we are designed. Truth be told, you may have been reading this as just a novel or devotional before bed or you may have been taking notes and cross referencing each verse. Or you may have even just been reading it from your own personal point of view and relating yourself to the people, my twists and turns, or even the verses. No matter how you are designed, we are not all going to be like Mary. Because as she pondered on this monumental moment in her life, you were not there. Although you may have experienced something to this degree and you can relate, your reaction is going to be different than hers. And listen to me, friend, that is good. Because if we were all like Mary, you and I would find ourselves feeling inadequate because something would be missing.

Scripture does not give an exact reason as to why this young woman is silent, but it does point out the matter of her heart. Mary's heart was set in the right posture, for she was not treasuring things of the world but rather the gift straight from God.

Can you imagine this moment for her? She is a young woman in her early years, just giving birth and holding her newborn Son in her arms. Truthfully, I might have been in shock and silent as well. And could you expect anything different?

Lovely encouragement:

Jesus was the Word, yet He did not speak.

I am rejoicing for Mary, as we all should, because that was a big moment in history. Remember, she left the town she lived in along with the friends and family she knew to head to Bethlehem with Joseph. I am sure she faced ridicule and bashing from those she knew. She lived out the journey just as James suggests us to do, "Consider it pure joy, my brothers and sisters, whenever you face trials of many kinds," all to help usher God's promise into the world. (See James 1:2.) Yet instead of pondering what life might have looked like, she chose to treasure the things happening right in front of her that would affect the future of man. And you and I can do the same!

As we continue reading on in Luke, you and I will see in verse 51, Mary did the very same thing again. However, at this moment, it is because she is seeing her Son doing His Father's business. I admire not only that Joseph is a man of no words in the Bible but also that we read about Mary being a woman of few words. Too often, we get in our heads and begin pondering our own thoughts about the situation rather than pondering what God has done and is doing. Honestly, anytime I think about Mary, I sense that she was a soft-spoken woman who trusted the Lord in such an intensifying way. She did not fret about the chaos around her. We are given a prime example of such as we see her pondering and not panicking. Now, I am not sure if she knew about what task she took on, but she remained peaceful while pondering.

Yes, Scripture goes into great detail to give the people who did not have the New Testament a chance to see what God would do, but do you really think Mary understood what was going to happen to the baby boy she was holding?

Questions I would like to ask Mary:

Did you know you were holding the man who would redeem the entire world?

Did it dawn on you that the tiny hand you were holding would heal the blind, raise the dead, and be pierced for our transgressions?

Did you know that your simple answer, "May your word to me be fulfilled" (Luke 1:38), lead you to teaching women of all ages to be obedient, even when they did not know what it would entail?

Did it ever cross your mind that when you said yes to God, you would have to say no to people?

Do you have any questions for Mary?

When I became a nanny years ago, I learned quite a bit from those tiny tots. I learned to be silly, have fun, and let loose. But I will tell you, the moments I hold close to my heart are the moments they taught me to slow down. In the midst of the scheduling, spontaneous milk spills, and food preparations, the moments of simplicity were the ones I remember most. I knew the little ones I watched growing up would one day grow up and do great things. But the sweet, tender moments were packed with pondering.

Let's look back over these two verses:

"But Mary treasured up all these things and pondered them in her heart. The shepherds returned, glorifying and praising God for all the things they had heard and seen, which were just as they had been told" (Luke 2:19–20).

I love these two verses because they give you a glimpse into the Spirit in which Mary lived. If you notice, at the beginning of verse 19 it starts with "But." That is because all the shepherds had gone off to tell what they had seen and heard, but Mary treasured every ounce of her time with Jesus as she possibly could. Because her heart and arms were filled with promises of God.

Lovely encouragement:

Mary focused not on the problem of the world but on the one who would one day save it.

Questions

What questions would you ask Mary?

DAY 19

PATIENCE AND PRAYER

Story time.

When the time came for the purification rites required by the Law of Moses, Joseph and Mary took Him to Jerusalem to present Him to the Lord (as it is written in the Law of the Lord, "Every firstborn male is to be consecrated to the Lord"), and to offer a sacrifice in keeping with what is said in the Law of the Lord: "a pair of doves or two young pigeons."

Now there was a man in Jerusalem called Simeon, who was righteous and devout. He was waiting for the consolation of Israel, and the Holy Spirit was on him. It had been revealed to him by the Holy Spirit that he would not die before he had seen the Lord's Messiah. Moved by the Spirit, he went into the temple courts. When the parents brought in the child Jesus to do for him what the custom of the Law required, Simeon took him in his arms and praised God, saying:

"Sovereign Lord, as You have promised, You may now dismiss Your servant in peace. For my eyes have seen Your salvation, which You have prepared in the sight of all nations: a light for revelation to the Gentiles, and the glory of Your people Israel."

The child's father and mother marveled at what was said about Him. Then Simeon blessed them and said to Mary, his mother: "This child is destined to cause the falling and rising of many in Israel, and to be a sign that will be spoken against, so that the thoughts of many hearts will be revealed. And a sword will pierce your own soul too."

There was also a prophet, Anna, the daughter of Penuel, of the tribe of Asher. She was very old; she had lived with her husband seven years after her marriage and then was a widow until she was eighty-four. She never left the temple but worshiped night and day, fasting and praying. Coming up to them at that very moment, she gave thanks to God and spoke about the child to all who were looking forward to the redemption of Jerusalem. (Luke 2:22–38.)

You and I just read a beautiful story straight from the Bible. Now, you have to admit, our Dad is an awesome storyteller. In this beautiful story, we are able to see when God gives us promises, He will in fact answer what He says He will do.

Lovely Encouragement:

God's promises are true, and He will indeed accomplish what He says He is going to do.

So, let's dive into the story and talk about it. Simeon and Anna were two people who spent their lives in prayer. Simeon was a devout man, and Anna was a thankful giver. Simeon was absolutely committed to the belief in not only God but also what He promised. While Anna committed herself to praying and fasting in the form of worship. I would like for us to begin taking these two people's lives and learning how each of them helped welcome Jesus into the town of Jerusalem. And in turn teach us how to lovingly welcome Him into our hearts.

The promise given to Simeon was that he would see God's salvation (Jesus), which God had prepared for all the nations to see. Could you imagine God giving you a promise and you holding onto that promise without letting go of it until it was fulfilled? Simeon was a man who did not let go of God's promise until it was in his hands. It is almost as if God is desiring for us as readers today to understand that He does in fact want us to experience His blessings, even if that means prolonging our lives for just one simple embrace. As Simeon held Jesus, the Savior and Light of the world, in his arms, He began talking to God about what his eyes were seeing and what the nations would see as well.

I know I have asked this before, but I will ask again. What are some of the promises God has given you?

_____

_____

_____

_____

When I am in my quiet time with God, sometimes I am not quiet. Truthfully, I call those "Daddy-Daughter dates." I enjoy reading the prayers of the people before me out loud. What about you? Do you enjoy saying prayers out loud, whether they are yours or of others? As I was reading Simeon's prayer, it was almost as if he never skipped a beat in his conversations with God.

You and I have read in the last eighteen days about three people who prayed the desires of their heart out loud. We are created and designed to speak about our desires to our Father. (See Psalm 37:4.) We are created to speak not only to God but also to others. And sometimes, those prayers get to be spoken out loud around those we admire.

Lovely Encouragement:

Pray out loud because you never know if someone nearby needs to hear your faith.

Now let's look ahead to a woman named Anna. This widowed woman is found at the temple, praying. When we go back and look at the passage that talks about her life, there is quite a bit to unpack. She is a woman who gave up her home, life, career, and future to spend her days and nights at the temple fasting and praying. Have you ever met a person who, once they lost it all, would sit at a temple (or wherever) and pray? She was most definitely living out what our brother-in-Christ Paul wrote about in Colossians 4, verse 2. This is one of those verses that you and I can cling to every day, and it says, "Devote yourselves to prayer, being watchful and thankful."

I am sure neither of them would have ever dreamt that the desires of their hearts through the form of prayer and worship would have ever been answered in this way. Just think about it, a babe wrapped in cloths traveling into Jerusalem with His parents to present Him to be consecrated to the Lord is now in the hands of a man who would not let go of a promise and is passing by the very women praying to see redemption. I think it is an absolutely beautiful live portrait of the fact that even when we do not understand how God is going to answer our prayers, we can expect His greatest blessings to come in the most unexpected ways—but remember you must also be expecting them to happen, it's called faith. (See Hebrews 11:1.)

Back to your desires. Did you write them down? I don't want to ask you how you think God will answer them. I actually want to ask you a deeper question. Do you believe God will answer your prayer? *No*, really, do you? Or do you do what the world is telling you to do, "fake it till you make it"? If you said yes, I am rejoicing and thanking God with you already! And if you said no, that is okay. Because sometimes we get in a place of doubt and believe the lie that our prayers and desires cannot be met. However, I do want to encourage you right here with this: when you are doubting, it might help to discipline your prayer life. I honestly don't think anyone can make a mistake in praying too much.

A few years back, I devoted myself to getting in my war room and locking myself in there for two hours. Every morning from 5:00 a.m. until 7:00 a.m., I would not let myself leave the room. There were mornings I would have to force myself out of bed because I was exhausted. Yet other times, I had to force myself out of the room, not because I wanted to share with you what I did. But rather share with you what God did with the time I gave Him.

Just like Anna gave up her home, possession, and time, I did the same. The dishes in the sink would still be there when I got there, along with the laundry and dirty floors. My time with my Abba was much more important. Especially since my heart was full of desires. It wasn't easy by any means. And I am sure it wasn't easy for Anna, but I figured if she would be blessed by having Jesus in her presence after giving it all up, what would I be able to hold if I did the same? I did it on the days I didn't want to, and I did it on the days I did want to. From my heart to yours, I am not telling you this story to boast. I am telling you this story to give you some encouragement and incentive. I want you to experience God like Anna, Mary, and myself.

Lovely Encouragement:

When we expect the blessing of God, we should also accept it, even if it is not what we expected.

I admire their proclamation and patience in prayer. It is a refresher, is it not? And I also have admiration for these two people who spent days on end in prayer and patience. It personally gives me hope that we can do the same. Simeon was only visiting the temple that day as a priest, while Anna was staying there night and day. However, both of them encountered Jesus, yet have different stories to tell of their encounter. And the same goes for you and me. You may just be visiting for the first time or have been on this journey for days on end, but that does not discount the interaction you have with Jesus. We worship the same living God, read the same Bible and memorize the same verses, worship Him to the same songs, but we are each going to have different encounters.

Lovely Encouragement:

There are going to be prayers that will take years
to be answered; remain in prayer and be patient.
The encouragement behind this is that when God is
allowing you to wait, He is indeed preparing the best
blessing He has prepared for you.

Question

» What was the promise God gave Simeon?

» How old was Anna?

» Do you think age has a limit on God's ability to come
through on His promises?

» Note to self: What you hear you may not always
understand; just give it some time.

139

Day 20

Come and Worship Him

"After Jesus was born in Bethlehem in Judea, during the time of King Herod, Magi from the east came to Jerusalem and asked, 'Where is the one who has been born King of the Jews? We saw his star when it rose and have come to worship him.'"

Matthew 2:1–2

As we remember from previous days, Jesus was born in a little place called Bethlehem, not Nazareth, because it had been prophesied by Micah: "But you, Bethlehem Ephrathah, though you are small among the clans of Judah, out of you will come for me one who will be ruler over Israel, whose origins are from of old, from ancient times" (Micah 5:2).

I am going to start off by asking a weird question. Have you ever been in a dark place, searching for light? Now that light might be the light of the fridge, and no judgment on my end! Nonetheless, it's dark, and you can't see. And the only thing on your mind is, "I wish I could see!" Say it's the middle of the night, you get out of bed only to find yourself in your dark home, and you think, *If I stub my toe, I am going to scream.* And as you're walking, you are doing that mummy walk, where your arms are stretched out in front of you, hoping you don't run into the wall, and your feet are doing the "shoe shuffle." Do you know what I mean?

According to Scripture, the people during the time of Jesus' birth were living in complete darkness. (See Isaiah 9:2.) People were searching for light. Just like you and I do! You might be wondering why the Bible would say, "People were walking in darkness." And the simplified version is because the enemy was at work and those who were inhabiting the land either had not remembered what their ancestors had said, or they were too overwhelmed with the emotions and the environment that they didn't know what to do. They, like many of us, were bogged down by the pressure and had little to no desire to change. That is one of the reasons God sent His Son—because He knew His creation was in the dark and needed a light.

So let me set the scene up for you. Men were traveling from a far-off land and searching for the home of where this star was leading them. They had been following it and now came to a little town called Bethlehem. There is no detail as to how many there were or where they came from specifically, other than from the east. Yet, we know they are traveling to see Jesus because they asked for the King who has been born of the Jews. I would like to show you a verse from the book of Numbers that may shed some light on this story:

"I see Him, but not now; I behold Him, but not near. A star will come out of Jacob; a scepter will rise out of Israel. He will crush the foreheads of Moab, the skulls of all the people of Sheth" (Numbers 24:17).

They may have entered the streets of the merchants and began asking those around them, "Where is the King?" And many very well could have pointed to the palace. But these men were not traveling long distances to see a King in power and of jealousy; they were searching for the King who was born of God's power and of the Jews.

Lovely Encouragement:

Power and pride, jealousy, and judging won't make you a king.

You see, these men, along with a few others, treasured up the Word of God in their hearts as Moses had instructed them. (See Deuteronomy 6.) Therefore, they knew this star they chose to follow was a sign from God to lead them to the King. They may have been Jewish astrologers who happened to be looking up and out into the sky and saw it, God may have sent a word to them to tell them to follow it, or the star may have appeared on their front doorstep. Many ideas and speculations can be made as to how their journey began, but no matter how it began, they chose to take the journey. They not only followed the commands of old but also this bright light. What leaps off the pages about these men is that they were wise enough to know the Word of God and look at His Word and know they would follow it to find a bundle of joy wrapped in cloths waiting to change the world.

Lovely Encouragement:

These men were not wise because they followed a star; they were wise because of their faith. You are wise when you follow God's wisdom, not man's ways.

God was so proud of His Son and desired to show Him off to everyone. Yet, He did not share the news with everyone at first. I am not sure why He didn't allow those who were near Jesus to come. It might have been that their hearts were uninviting and their homes were still closed. However, you have these men who lived hundreds, maybe even thousands of miles away, receive something they had been waiting on for a long time while in the dark. And to think it had been over four hundred years since God spoke to His creation, and they trusted what their ancestors and the Torah had said about the Messiah coming.

Faith-filled fun fact: The Torah is the first five books in the Bible. The Torah is a teaching revealed to Moses from God on Mount Sinai (Genesis, Exodus, Leviticus, Numbers, and Deuteronomy).

Instead of God sending these men angels as He did with Mary, Joseph, and the shepherds, He went with a different approach. He sent them a light. A light to show them the way through the darkness. But not just any light. No, no, no. This was not a light that was plugged into a Christmas tree or fridge. This light was a star moving like a lure to show them the way to go. And they followed it to do what? Worship.

I could go into a great detailed spin-off and ask questions like: (1) Why did these men follow a random star? (2) Why did the star move? (3) Did they ever try to touch it? (4) Did they know where they were going? (5) Did God tell them to follow the star?

But I want to stick to the facts. The fact is these men followed a star that led to Jesus. And when they arrived, they said, "Where is the one who has been born king of the Jews? We saw His star when it rose and have come to worship Him."

COME AND WORSHIP HIM

Questions

» Who do you worship?

» How do you worship? Check out this verse in Romans 12, verse 1, "Therefore, I urge you, brothers and sisters, in view of God's mercy, to offer your bodies as a living sacrifice, holy and pleasing to God—this is your true and proper worship."

» So, let me ask you another question about worship. What is true worship?

» If you said giving up all that you are, you are correct. But there is more! Being a living sacrifice is what is true worship. Yes, the songs are great, and when the beta hits, you feel your soul jump, and you enjoy it. However, there is so much more.

» I tend to find myself worrying sometimes when I should be worshiping. Do you do the same?

» What challenge could you and I give each other to allow ourselves to be vulnerable in the midst of worship? Even if it takes a while to find the place (feeling, emotion) to get there.

» Can I challenge you to do something? Spend one day in prayer. Whenever you find yourself at a place to make a decision, talk to God. Whenever a problem arises, talk to God. When something good happens, talk to God. Just try it for one day. You have so many other days in your life not to, why not spend one day talking to your Abba? It's just a challenge, and I have faith you can do it!

Day 21

Be Delighted, Not Disturbed

When King Herod heard this he was disturbed, and all Jerusalem with him. When he had called together all the people's chief priests and teachers of the law, he asked them where the Messiah was to be born. "In Bethlehem in Judea," they replied, "for this is what the prophet has written: 'But you, Bethlehem, in the land of Judah, are by no means least among the rulers of Judah; for out of you will come a ruler who will shepherd my people Israel.'"

As the question traveled back to King Herod from the wandering wise men, he began to feel disturbed—some translations say troubled or greatly agitated. Why was King Herod expressing such negative feelings? Well, he had just been asked by men from a far-off land where the King was, and due to his prideful heart, he did not want to accept the fact that they were not asking about him. Now, I am by no means taking King Herod's side on any of this matter, but I am learning to place my feet in other people's shoes or sandals, if we may. Can you imagine how he must have felt that day? He had been ruling Judea for years at this point. Life was going great; I am sure there were complications like any place that has a leader, but nonetheless, King Herod was comfortable with his position, and so were some of the people in the land. In his mind, he may have been thinking he was doing a decent job as king. That's typically what pride will allow you to do.

Yet, in one full sweep of a sentence, his whole life had changed. They say a baby changes everything. And I cannot even begin to imagine what he must have been thinking or feeling in this unforgettable, monumental moment.

Many times we let pride get in the way of doing what is pleasing to the Lord. And truthfully, I am right there with you. I would like to tell you that I am the most humble person I know, but that is not true. Some days, I am prideful. And King Herod gives us a quick glimpse into how pride will keep you on the throne. But Jesus is the living proof that we are supposed to be off the throne, humbling ourselves. After all, He came into this world with absolutely nothing, was wrapped in cloths, and then hung on a cross wearing only our sins. I cannot think of a more fitting example of who to let be on the throne of our hearts.

Lovely Encouragement:

Pride sits you on the throne. Humility sends you to the throne room.

The teachers of the law during this time had to have known not only the Torah but also the prophecies that had been spoken over the years. One of those being Micah 5:2, which says, "But you, Bethlehem Ephrathah, though you are small among the clans of Judah, out of you will come for Me One who will be ruler over Israel, whose origins are from of old, from ancient times." But there was still something that gave them a death grip on the throne. What was it? Was it the power they had? The control? Could it be the feeling of letting go of what they built up for so many years or the sense of entitlement they felt while they were in control? Or could it have been the fact that a baby had just been born, and they thought this was a disruption of their plan? As I learn more about King Herod, I learn more about myself. And I hope you will do the same.

Lovely Encouragement:

Great power alongside pride does not win you great favor.

We are all facing a great power that we cannot see. Some of us are able to feel it or sense it. But either way, now that you know, there is a war going on for the throne, around us, and even within us. The enemy wants to win, and he will attempt any form of temptation or trial to lure you to take dominance of the throne. He has been doing it for years and knows how to stab your faith and heart. Believe me when I say this, the enemy knows Scripture and what God says. You don't have to travel too far into Scripture before you see him tempt God's creation using God's words.

The enemy, as said by a great friend, comes only to steal, kill, and destroy. (See John 10:10.) The enemy was stealing the joy of the people who could have welcomed in the Messiah by allowing fear to result in jealousy and pride. And let me remind you, dear friend, jealousy (comparison) is the thief of joy. And the truth of the matter is, God knew it was going to be this way. He gave man free will to decide whether we were going to let pride take a seat or find humiliation at His feet.

King Herod claimed to be a God-worshiper, but he was lying. God does not like it when you are lukewarm, and He promises that He will spit you out if you are. (See Revelation 3:16). How often do we take a hold of the arms of the throne and hold on tightly because we are terrified as to what will happen if we let go?

Joy vs. Comparison
Worship vs. Control
Pride vs. Humility

I urge you, my dear friend, there is a war in your hearts and minds to take dominance over the throne. Don't let the enemy win, and don't let the enemy in. He knows the way to stab your faith and your heart and that is through using God's people and manipulating your minds. If King Herod had humbled himself, he would have rightfully gotten off his throne and given it to Jesus, King of the Jews. But he didn't. I hope you learned from this story of King Herod. God is not in the lukewarm, prideful business. He wants your heart to be accompanied by Him. And I have to confess, it's hard to surrender to God, but it will get easier in time if you start now! Be open and organic with your Father! He loves that kind of stuff!

Lovely Encouragement:

Stray away from a haughty heart and
humble yourself before the Lord.
Use kind words to others.
Encourage one another in words and actions.
Defend your faith with passion and purpose.
When you feel yourself getting prideful because
you're sitting on the throne, get up and get down.

Questions

» Imagine you are in a room where you are placed on a throne. A throne where you decide what happens in the day. What are your thoughts, feelings, emotions, and desires? Go ahead; take time and list them.

» Are you willing to release your white knuckles from the arms of the throne to let your Father take over?

» Quick and deep question. Do you trust God?

» I know the question above is answered with many twists and turns. But what is keeping you strapped to the seat? There can be more than one answer.

» Why are you terrified to let go?

Prayer: Father, most gracious Father who blesses us with friends, emotions, and desires. You have flooded our hearts and land with your glorious creation. And I am ever grateful for it. I need your help. It is hard for me to ask for this, but I need your help getting myself off the throne of my life. You are the Creator of every thought, desire, and emotion, and I desire to align whatever I have inside of me with You. I have made a list of what occupies Your throne. If there is anything in Your seat, I give You permission to remove it from not only my heart but also my life. I need more space for You and the Holy Spirit. Thank You for being patient with me all these years as I have packed all these earthly possessions on Your throne. Come help me and do it ever so gently. I thank You, Father, for helping me. I pray all of this in the name of Jesus.

Amen.

DAY 22

MANIPULATION IS NOT A WISE MOVE

"Then Herod called the Magi secretly and found out from them the exact time the star had appeared. He sent them to Bethlehem and said, 'Go and search carefully for the child. As soon as you find him, report to me, so that I too may go and worship him.'"

Matthew 2:7–8

Have you ever taken control of a situation in order to get your way? I know I have. It isn't the most fun to admit. But we are friends here, and I am being open and organic with you, friend! There is a name for that, and it is manipulation. It's when you take a situation you don't particularly like or something you don't really want to do, so you "ask" people to rearrange their actions or plans to make it happen in your favor.

Now, I am all about asking friends for help, but the problem begins when the motive of the heart is not fully expressed in the mission. A prime example of such a collaboration would be planning a wedding, working on a school project, or performing with a team to obtain a certain goal. However, what we see here in this story about King Herod is that he was far from wanting to work together as a team to worship the newborn King. In fact, he wanted to know the whereabouts of Jesus the newborn King so he could murder Him.

Let me set the scene for you. In a hidden room in the castle stands King Herod with men from a far-off land. They had been led here by a star to see the newborn King. By surprise to King Herod (the King of Judea), it was not him they wanted to see. So he began asking the men questions. More than likely, he asked how far they had traveled, where they came from, where they were going, when they first saw the star, and more. As the King pleased the men with words using his silver tongue. All because his request was filtered through a wrong motive. As we read on ahead, we will see the motive of his heart that was hidden behind the request. (See Matthew 2:16.)

Do you remember on Day 21 when we talked about King Herod not wanting to get off the throne? Not only had King Herod not wanted to leave his throne, but now we see him trying to manipulate the situation in order to stay on it. Truthfully, I believe he had an idol problem. Little did King Herod know that the newborn King did not need an earthly throne to sit upon.

Let me ask you, do you think King Herod was jealous, and that is why he was being manipulative? I think he was. And I don't think it was just the "throne" he was desiring. It may have been the power and the applause from man. You and I idolize materials and emotions in this world, and it is truly a battle we face every day.

I remember being between a rock and a hard place many times in my life. One time in particular was when I felt the Lord prompting me to step away from teaching at church. Now, this decision did not come easy. I sure did fight God on it. But nonetheless, I was faced with a decision of do I stay here where I feel comfortable or do I surrender the position and trust the Lord. You see, not only had I been asked to be placed in this position, it was not something I sought out to do. Yes, I have my degree in teaching, but my degree was not in disciple-making. In fact, I had no clue what I was doing when I started teaching. Day after day, for about three or four months, I refused to let my position go. Finally, after many prayers and tears, I gave in. I stopped trying to manipulate the situation and stay "in reign" and on the throne. I graciously bowed. I am not sure if King Herod was anything like me where he had a moment with God and was told he would teach many generations, but I did.

I tell you this small little story to encourage you to step away from what you are holding so tightly to in this season while you are in His seat. As I am writing to you, I have not been filled with another ministry position, but I have been given the blessing of more time to be fed. Not every story has to do with making hasty decisions, but every story has to do with our hearts. The king was quick to come up with a plan to remain in reign, but due to the mixture of his heart and the prophecy, he would not be able to stay where he was.

Lovely Encouragement:

It is up to you to decide if you are willing to stop trying to come up with schemes, plans, and ideas to manipulate your story.

Bonus talk: As I was rereading this day before sending it off to the editor for the first time, I had a realization. Had I stuck with teaching in the ministry at church, I would not have been able to give ample time or attention to writing this book for you. It is because God knew what He was doing when He allowed the door of that classroom to be opened for the last time and for me to walk through to the next adventure in my life. So many times, we ask God to open doors for us to walk into something, but how often do we allow ourselves to trust God when He opens the door for us to leave?

Questions

» What have you personally learned about King Herod?

» What are similar and opposing character traits between Jesus and King Herod?

» Out of those character traits, where do you find yourself leaning more toward? (If you lean more towards King Herod, no worries, you are not alone.)

Follow me along with this prayer as we renew our minds:

Father, in Your Son's holy name, I am thankful for You. I am thankful that You have allowed me to prosper and be in good health all according to Your plan. I have the mind of Christ, and I align the thoughts, feelings, and desires of His heart. I submit my mind to You. And I expose my mind to You so that I can be made new. I disapprove of any arguments, theories, tactics, reasoning, or proud things in my mind that sets me up against the flesh. For it is not against the flesh and blood. I know it is against what I cannot see. Therefore, it is against my mind and the very thoughts that come into it. I want my mind to be at peace. Grant me peace of mind. I am now transformed by the renewing of my mind in the way I know how. I approve of any good, acceptable, perfect, true, noble, right, lovely, admirable, and praiseworthy, all according to Your will. I roll my works upon You, Father, and I commit my mind to You. When I begin to drift, allow the Holy Spirit to guide me back to Truth, Your Truth, which is the pulling down of strongholds. Thank You, Father, for establishing Your plans in my life for my good and Your glory.

In Jesus' name I pray, amen.

DAY 23

DROP IT AND LEAVE IT

After they had heard the king, they went on their way, and the star they had seen when it rose went ahead of them until it stopped over the place where the child was. When they saw the star, they were overjoyed. On coming to the house, they saw the child with his mother Mary, and they bowed down and worshiped him. Then they opened their treasures and presented him with gifts of gold, frankincense and myrrh. And having been warned in a dream not to go back to Herod, they returned to their country by another route.

Matthew 2:9–12

It is so fascinating to me that, in the beginning of creation, God created light and called it "good." And here we see men following a light to God's own Son, the Light of the world. There is no coincidence in how this story played out. Matthew was a meticulous man, especially when it came to writing about the life of Jesus. And God, well, He is the only one who can write a story so well creating and weaving pieces of His creation to tie up for us the most beautiful and glorious gifts from the beginning of creation and all throughout it. Just think about it. We have a Father who loves us so dearly, and the best way for Him to be a part of His creation was for Him to come into it.

God not only created light, but He became the Light in the dark world so we can finally see like Him. (See Genesis 3:4 and 1 John 1:5–7.) As Matthew was writing about these men, he not only expressed their faithfulness to follow a star but also their joyfulness as they arrived at their destination. Not too many people like to harp on emotions, but I sure am glad Matthew did.

I am not sure if you have trekked a journey for miles on end, but whether you have or not, these men could have expressed any emotion from their journey, but they chose to express joyfulness. Matthew points out to us not only their *emotions* but the *motive* behind what pushed them to keep going along in the journey. So, what was their main focus on this mission to see the King? Their main focus was to worship the King. We talked in previous days about what worship truly is—being a living sacrifice to God. Did any of that shock you or did you already have that knowledge?

We often go to church, though we may not have traveled for miles like these men, carrying our burdens, blames, baggage, and busy minds. Nonetheless, we carry it into the house of the Lord with us. But my question to you is, what do you and I do with those things when we get there?

We wake up early to get our best face, clothes, and attitude on, but deep down, we might have a heart that is not at its best. We then arrive at the church building, we greet others with our best face forward, and the conversations sometimes go like this: "Hello and good morning. How are you today?" You may reply with, "I am good, thank you for asking." And then the conversation is over. You walk into the sanctuary with your baggage, burdens and busy mind. You might be thinking, *If I can just get to the sanctuary, I will have made it.* You accomplished your task for the week. You might be eager to sing and be taught the Word of God in hopes that your week will look better than the days past. And for what, to be charged up for one hour? But my more pressing question to you is what do you and I do with those things we carried there? Do we pack them up in our purse or Bible bag and head right back out the door we came in?

Lovely Encouragement:

What you carry into the house of the Lord can in fact be left there for good.

As I started studying these men, I noticed two qualities about them that I did not obtain in my journey; faithfulness and joyfulness. I will be honest with you: as I would attend church faithfully, sing in the choir, lead in the ministries, and serve in the community, my heart was not like these men. It was a hard year for me when I began to lose hope. Truth be told, I was absolutely numb for about three months prior to losing it all. When I did finally start to experience the emotions of loss, I felt everything. And you may have experienced the same. I was talking to a friend the other night and we touched on the base of *positivity*. And how it can change your *perspective*. Believe me when I say, I understand. It is not always easy being positivity. And the truth is, you cannot always be positive. But what you can do is change your perspective about the situation at hand. Take a look at these men. They could have grumbled their entire journey, like some men you and I have read about! (See Numbers 14). But they chose to be joyful!

So I studied these men, and I noticed a pattern with them.

Now, they did not have to repeat the *pattern*, but we as Christians might want to try it out. They followed God, asked questions, found Jesus, presented their best to Him, and then went back home. I truly believe these men were living out the words from Psalm 16:11. Check this out: "You make known to me the path of life; You will fill me with joy in Your presence, with eternal pleasures at Your right hand."

Now, I want to encourage you, faithful and joyful friend, along your journey. There are going to be trials, temptations, and even tribulations that come your way. There are going to be good and goofy distractions that postpone your journey. But that's okay. Even Jesus came for one mission, and along His journey, He danced, prayed, dined, and served. He could have come into the world, completed the one task His Father commanded, and then done a reverse swan dive back to heaven. But He didn't. Jesus stayed and soaked up His time with His creation so He could teach us how to truly and properly worship the Father. It was not by the *works* He did or the *words* He said; it was His *welcoming* heart to all who wanted to *worship*.

I lead a small discipleship and generational Scripture memory group, and I requested both groups to memorize Romans 12:1–2. I desire for them to know the Word of God and how to properly worship Him. Paul writes to the Romans and for us today, and it says,

DROP IT AND LEAVE IT

Therefore, I urge you, brothers and sisters, in view of God's mercy, to offer your bodies as a living sacrifice, holy and pleasing to God—this is your true and proper worship. Do not conform to the pattern of this world, but be transformed by the renewing of your mind. Then you will be able to test and approve what God's will is—His good, pleasing and perfect will.

The Magi knew how to worship, but King Herod did not. Instead of barging back into the King's home after their time of worshiping the son of God, they traveled back to their homes because, more than likely, they knew that if they had returned to the king, he would have them killed for not worshiping him. Yet, they were given strict orders by a king to return and give the whereabouts of the new King, but they chose to listen to God and obey His commands. They chose to worship and walk out over their life, more than likely to spare them their lives.

Lovely Encouragement:

You can be *positive* on your *path* based off the *perspective* you *possess*!

Questions

» When do you worship the Father, Son, and Holy Spirit? Is it only on Sunday mornings or Wednesday nights? Is it at the breakfast table, dinner table, or even when you're preparing your meals? When do you worship the one who walked into your darkness and delivered you?

» How often do you lay all your worldly treasures at His feet? I am not just talking about saying, "God, this is too much to handle. Please take it!" I am talking about laying up your treasures here on earth in preparation for heaven.

» Are you leaving room for the Holy Spirit to lead you through the day? Are you allowing yourself to be filled with the presence of God first rather than the presence of people or the world?

» Real question: Are you willing to let the Holy Spirit lead you?

» Would you follow Him wherever He goes? Just as the Magi were led to a far-off land from a far distance, would you go great lengths with God being led by Him? Examples: school, work, home, practices, mission trips, neighbor's house, church, etc.

Day 24

Follow in Obedience

When they had gone, an angel of the Lord appeared to Joseph in a dream. "Get up," he said, "take the child and his mother and escape to Egypt. Stay there until I tell you, for Herod is going to search for the child to kill him." So he got up, took the child and his mother during the night and left for Egypt, where he stayed until the death of Herod. And so was fulfilled what the Lord had said through the prophet: "Out of Egypt I called my son." When Herod realized that he had been outwitted by the Magi, he was furious, and he gave orders to kill all the boys in Bethlehem and its vicinity who were two years old and under, in accordance with the time he had learned from the Magi.

Matthew 2:13–16

It's Christmas Eve, and you have been following Love Himself through the pages of His journey and of yours and mine. It has been so nice unpacking these simple Truths to you and revealing His story to you on a deeper level. When I set out to write a book, it did not start with that intent in mind. In fact, it started the night of Thanksgiving. When the Lord revealed to me the journey of Jesus coming into the world. I was eager to share with my many friends, but I just did not know how or when. Many nights had passed, and on November 30, my Father quietly whispered, "You will write a book starting tomorrow." I was a bit overwhelmed, but I trusted Him.

I woke up the next morning and began the journey. I did not have the editors I have today, nor the audience I have today, but what I did have was the willingness to obey His command. Each morning at 5:00 a.m., sometimes earlier, I would wake up and share the next day's journey with my groups. I was eager and intentional with each day as it pertained to His story and the many people who walked before Him who had a hand in ushering Him into the world. As I studied Scripture, more information would flood my mind about what they felt, experienced, saw, and expressed. It was almost too much to text, but I did it. And let me tell you why I did it. It was for the simple fact that I experienced joy in what I was learning, and I desired the same for others.

I just want to congratulate you one more time and say Merry Christmas Eve. Today we pick up where Joseph, Mary, and Jesus are picking up their lives and traveling onward in obedience. King Herod is once again showing us how not to be, but this time he is not just a man of words but a man who is at work. I truly believe the enemy was a part of this plan. The enemy is always trying to prevent God from working.

But before any harm could come to His Son, God sent an angel to tell Joseph to get up and take his family to Egypt. I want to let you in on something cool that you and I just noticed. The angel that appears to God is the same angel who appeared to the apostles when they were in jail and told them to get up, go, and continue preaching the Word of God. (See Acts 16:16–28.)

Lovely Encouragement:

God is all about getting His kingdom into creation, and He will stop at no man, jail, or haughty heart to have the final say.

You see, King Herod was furious because, as mentioned before, there was someone coming to take away his power, authority, and throne. So he sent troops into the towns and killed every boy under the age of two. And the reason he chose that age is that he had studied what the Magi had revealed to him about their journey. It had taken them about two years to reach Jesus. So he based his search for this new King, and instead of guessing who it could be and questioning the whole town, he made the decision to have them killed. Again, that is why I truly believe the enemy was behind this. It is not right to decide to end someone else's life. But as we know, the enemy is out to steal, *kill*, and destroy. So, do you think his manipulating mind was behind this?

So out of obedience, Joseph once again packs up his family and heads to Egypt. I don't necessarily like to question God, but ever so often, I question what is going to happen next. And instead of God giving Joseph an idea of what He was going to do, He simply said, "Stay there until I tell you." Personally, I get bored with waiting. Sometimes aggravated and agitated. Maybe it is because I enjoy being on the go. But here again, we see Joseph do exactly what he is told to do with no rebuttal.

As mentioned before, I did not go out and seek to write. In fact, the majority of what I write is Spirit-led, and I would prefer it to be that way. Because if it were up to me, my life, mind, and soul would be a chaotic circus. And most days, when I am not being obedient listening to my Father and allowing Him to make decisions for me, I do tend to be more overwhelmed and agitated in a negative way.

So my encouragement to you on this beautiful day the Lord has made for us, go enjoy your friends and family. Enjoy the journey that you have walked so far, but just remember, this is not the end of your story. Your story is still being written. Will you allow Him to write your story and lead you through the chapters of your life? If so, follow along with me in this prayer:

Prayer: Dear Dad, in Your Son's precious and holy name, I commit myself to walk alongside You through this journey. Thank You for sending Your Word into the world. Your Word is living, and it produces in me fruits of Your spirit. You have sent Your Word here into earth and into my heart. I give it permission to dwell in me and begin producing much fruit. I will meditate on it day and night as I have seen others before me do. Continue to protect me and guide me from the harmful enemy. It has been said in Your Word that a powerful man of this earth went to great lengths to attempt to kill Your Son. Send Your angel of armies to my side and protect me as You did Your Son. I confidently stand by Your Word, and I establish it in my heart and mind. Amen.

DAY 25

IT'S NOT JUST ANY STORY; IT'S HIS STORY

"The Word became flesh and made his dwelling among us. We have seen his glory, the glory of the one and only Son, who came from the Father, full of grace and truth."

(John 1:14)

When the text says, "The Word became flesh," it means that in a literal sense. When God spoke light into existence on the first day, there was no mention of the sun, moon, or stars. Aren't those sources of light? So how could light be in existence before the sources of light existed? It couldn't have been a lightbulb because electricity hadn't been invented yet. So what was this light? Simple answer, Jesus.

By God speaking light into existence, not only did the Light become light, but it also became His Word. Then that very same Light became flesh. Do you see where I am going? God already had His Son within Him because it says so in Scripture (Genesis 1:1–3).

Jesus Christ became the greatest example for us. But what is so fascinating to me about the whole story is that before Jesus did a single miracle, spoke a single word, or walked a step, He was God. It is hard for us to comprehend when truth is staring at you right in the face as it did with Mary. There is no denying the *love* of our Father.

When I was in elementary, middle, and even high school, I used to leave my house to get on the bus. And everyday, as I was running down the driveway, I would hear from my home my mom yelling, "Tell someone about Jesus." And although I knew she meant that in the literal sense, she also meant I needed to act, say, do as Jesus did. And what are we to act, say, and do to be more like Jesus Christ? We read about Him each time we open the Bible. But if you are anything like me, sometimes you get lost in the story; you don't always see the Messiah within the message.

We have been learning quite a bit about different people and their journeys. Yet, have you stopped to see the resemblance of these people in correlation to Jesus Christ? All of these people we have read about these past twenty-four days did not know who Jesus was going to be. They knew a few things like how He would be born (see Isaiah 7:14) and where He would be born (Micah 5:2), but they had no idea who He would be or what all He would do. He would grow up to be compassionate, caring, and giving. He was a leader, preacher, listener, and more! He would heal the lame, give blind their sight, and deliver people from demons. You and I sometimes go through droughts and dry seasons, and we forget that those stories are real. They aren't just told to be talked about. They are told to be remembered!

I am sure that Anna, Simeon, Elizabeth, Zechariah, John, Joseph, the shepherds, and even the Magi all hoped that Jesus would grow up and be brave and courageous, patient and kind, loving and genuine, which He did. But He surpassed what they thought He could do.

Every parent wants the best for their children. But I am sure none of those who came to see Jesus or grew up with Him knew the great miracles He would perform, missions He would go on, or lives He would save. They had no idea that His hands, the very hands they played ball with and cleaned the table off after dinner, would one day break bread for over thousands of men, women, and children using five loaves of bread and two small fish, Jesus surpassed their way of thinking.

Lovely Encouragement:

God genuinely wants the same for YOU, His child!

Remember this holiday season that yes, the gifts are nice, the food is tasty, and the people are fun, but this is a moment in time to reflect the fullness of God and man in the flesh. It's a wonderful Christmas story, but more than that, this is Christ's story!

Merry Christmas, friend! Enjoy *today*!

DAY 26

PEACE

"Peace I leave with you; My peace I give you. I do not give to you as the world gives. Do not let your hearts be troubled and do not be afraid."

John 14:27

Have you ever been on a scavenger hunt? You know those good ol' fashioned treasure hunts that send you around your home, neighborhood, or even town? Well, I want to encourage you with something, just like shepherds followed what the angels said, the Magi followed a moving star, you followed your way through both my story and Scripture, you found a treasure.

Today is a day to reflect on the Hostess with the mostest. And that is your Abba. The one who gave you His one and only Son. So you can be *present* with Him and be at *peace* all the days of your life.

Not only that but also to reflect on what you have learned about the real-life, emotional, inspirational people in the Bible.

Mary: obedient, set apart (holy), and determined.

Joseph: afraid turned faithful, obedient to God's Word and command.

Elizabeth: understanding, tuned into God (Elohim), a listener and a worshiper.

Zechariah: doubtful turned confident, silent, but yet observing and absorbing.

The Magi: trusting, obedient, faithful, and willing to go the extra mile to seek out Jesus.

The Shepherds: first missionaries and willing to leave their sheep (career) behind to see what God had done.

The angels: obedient.

You can reflect all of these characteristics of God too! Are you willing, able, and making yourself available?

Questions

» Which character(s) from this journey do you think you are most like? Tell me why.

» Which character(s) from this journey do you think you are least like? Tell me why.

» Which character(s) from this journey do you want to strive to be more like? Tell me why.

Please don't miss out on this last challenge. Go and tell your Abba, "Thank You" for blessing you with the sweetest and most pure gift of all, Himself!

ABOUT THE AUTHOR

Courtney Grisham, a forgiven, redeemed, and set-free twenty-five-year-old with a passion for sharing the Good News, grew up in a loving home where Jesus was exalted. After running from the truth for years and into the arms of a man who was not right for her, she finally found salvation, and out of that, this first devotional book was born. Courtney writes about her life experiences and how they intertwine with the Gospel of Jesus Christ.

CPSIA information can be obtained
at www.ICGtesting.com
Printed in the USA
BVHW031808141222
654220BV00010B/436